Making an Issue of Child Abuse

Political Agenda Setting for Social Problems

Barbara J. Nelson

The University of Chicago Press • Chicago and London

BARBARA J. NELSON is associate professor
at the Hubert H. Humphrey Institute of
Public Affairs, the University of Minnesota. She was recently a visiting fellow at
the Russell Sage Foundation.

The University of Chicago Press, Chicago 60637
The University of Chicago Press, Ltd., London

© 1984 by the University of Chicago
All rights reserved. Published 1984
Printed in the United States of America
91 90 89 88 87 86 85 84   5 4 3 2

LIBRARY OF CONGRESS CATALOGING IN PUBLICATION DATA

Nelson, Barbara J., 1949–
   Making an issue of child abuse.

   Includes bibliographical references and index.
   1. Child abuse—Government policy—United States.
I. Title.
HV741.N39   1984   362.7′044   83-18044
ISBN 0-226-57200-5

To Tom Lindenfeld
and in memory of
Oliver Dorigan Nelson

Contents

Preface

I remember quite vividly when I first became interested in how the problem of child abuse became a public policy issue. In 1974, as a Mershon Public Policy Intern at the Ohio State University, I worked on a project investigating how hospitals respond to child abuse cases. My task was to write a questionnaire which would elucidate how and when hospitals determine that a child has been maltreated. I had a fair amount of experience writing questionnaires but knew nothing about child abuse. It seemed sensible to go straight to the reference room to remedy this lack.

There I was confronted by a startling finding. An examination of the *Readers' Guide to Periodical Literature* and the *Social Science and Humanities Index* showed that absolutely no articles on child abuse (regardless of what term one used) had been published before 1962. Later research in other indexes proved me slightly wrong, but at that moment I was surprised and intrigued by the finding. Certainly some parents had always treated their children brutally. Why hadn't anyone written about it before 1962? What happened in 1962 to make abuse newsworthy? What transformed a condition into a social problem, and a social problem into a policy issue?

These questions piqued my interest so thoroughly that I decided to do research on agenda setting. The question became, Which issue or issues should I choose? The more I read about child abuse, the more I was convinced that doing a series of case studies on abuse would answer many of my more general questions about policy initiation. Child abuse had achieved several governmental agendas over a twenty-year period. The problem first came to the attention of public officials in 1955, when the American Humane Association shared its new research on abuse with the U.S. Children's Bureau. The Bureau's concern, aided by media attention, spurred state legislatures to pass child abuse reporting laws, and congressional interest soon followed. Here was a good example of intergovernmental influences on agenda setting, a subject all but absent from the agenda-setting literature.

The child abuse case added to the work on agenda setting in other ways as well. Much of the previous research had examined how technological change encouraged government to adopt new issues. Child abuse, on the other hand, was not a new problem, merely a newly recognized one. Moreover, child abuse was emblematic of a great deal of social policy making in America. In a country with no popularly successful socialist tradition and little public support for redistribution, there seemed to be a need for research on smaller, categorical programs where group demands for special social intervention are met. In addition, this issue allowed me to investigate how the state constructs and maintains the boundary between the public and private spheres through the manipulation of widely cherished symbols. Altogether, child abuse was a very compelling issue on which to base my study.

I brought my interests in agenda setting and child abuse to Princeton. With the support of the Daniel and Florence Guggenheim Research Program in Criminal Justice, directed by Jameson Doig, I was able to begin my research. My objective was to discover and reconstruct how individuals became concerned about the problem and how they mobilized their institutions to respond. The process of discovery and reconstruction was both exhilarating and exhausting. In trips to Denver, Chicago, New York, Boston, and Washington, D.C., the written records were located. These records took many forms—unpublished memos, correspondence, and reports, as well as books and journal articles. As always, the search was full of adventures. In the middle of research, one hard-pressed agency was contemplating destroying all but its most current records, and another discovered its historical records filed in a long-forgotten storeroom!

In addition, I interviewed fifty-two people who participated in setting the agendas under study. The interviews, which lasted from thirty minutes to twelve hours (over several days), were conducted with past and present high-ranking officials in the executive branch, members of Congress, congressional staff members, noted researchers, professors, legal and medical practitioners in the child abuse field, and national leaders in relevant private charity groups. The interviews focused on individuals who participated in setting the public agenda, sometimes to the exclusion of people who established or ran interesting programs. In addition, I interviewed a number of people whom I felt could or should have participated in setting particular agendas. This strategy paid handsome dividends in expanding my understanding of the structural barriers to access to public officials.

The interviews were semistructured and were conducted in three different ways. In most instances I conducted the interview, aided by an assistant who took detailed, often verbatim notes. On a few occasions, I conducted the interviews alone, and on fewer still, the interviews were taped and transcribed. The decision on which method to use was made on purely pragmatic grounds. Most people felt more at ease and were probably more candid when not confronted by a tape recorder. With very few exceptions (two to be exact), the individuals interviewed were open, helpful, and blessedly generous.

A word is in order on the use of quotations in this book. In his book, *A Government of Strangers*, Hugh Heclo posited a wonderful rule about quoting informants—no speakers were ever identified "even when they wanted to be."[1] That rule, appealing for its protection of the participants but perhaps disturbing to some readers, has not been used. Instead a more difficult rule has been substituted. All quotations remain anonymous unless there is public, documentary evidence which substantially says the same thing. This rule was chosen to create a balance between the protection of participants and the need for historical detail.

The carefully crafted words of three people sustained me while I wrote this book, and this triumvirate—unlikely though it is—deserves special mention. For encouragement in the labor of writing, I would like to acknowledge Anatole Broyard, Jimmy Breslin, and the late Anne Sexton.

Barbara J. Nelson

Acknowledgments

Although it is not customary, I would like to thank my loved ones as the first order of business. With gratitude I thank my family, Betty-Jane, Beverly, Murray, Michael, Barney, and Rachel, for their love and support. My deepest gratitude and love go to Tom Lindenfeld, who was there from beginning to end.

The project was interrupted for two years by a disabling illness. It is a testimony to the patience and skill of Dr. Donald Hoskins that I was able to complete this book. My heartfelt thanks go to him.

This work was generously supported from several sources. The Daniel and Florence Guggenheim Research Program in Criminal Justice, directed by my friend and colleague Jim Doig, supported the work for several years. It is expensive to do policy research requiring in-depth interviewing, and the Research Program in Criminal Justice was unstinting in its generosity. I would also like to acknowledge a grant from the Geraldine R. Dodge Foundation to the Center for New Jersey Affairs which supported my research one summer and allowed me to do the case study of New Jersey's child abuse reporting law. I would like to thank Ingrid Reed for her assistance in acquiring the Dodge Foundation Grant. Donald E. Stokes, Dean of the Woodrow Wilson School of Public and International Affairs at Princeton University, also generously made available faculty research resources through the School. My thanks go to all these people and institutions.

The Princeton University professional library staff is outstanding. I would like to acknowledge the special help of Jean Aroeste, Kevin Berry, Mary George, Rosemary Little, Linda Oppenheim, and Carol Tobin.

I would also like to thank the Princeton students and staff who worked with me on this project as research assistants. Their good humor and hard work made my task easier. My thanks go to Zaida Dillon, Missy Dungan, Laura Forese, Carla Hesse, Faye Kessin, Kirstie McClure, Lynn Meskill, Kathy Milton, Gabrielle Simms, and Amanda Thornton. I would like to acknowledge the special contributions of Denise Antolini and Mandy Carver, who provided "fugitive footnote" services in the last days of the work.

Many of my colleagues have offered helpful comments or assistance, as well as timely encouragement. I would especially like to thank Jameson W. Doig, Stanley Katz, Walter Murphy, Jerry Webman, and Julian Wolpert at Princeton University; Jack Walker and John Kingdon at the University of Michigan; Harold Wechsler at the University of Chicago; and Lynn Gordon at the University of Rochester. Several people active in the world of public affairs also read parts of the manuscript, giving me the benefit of their special knowledge of their institutions.

The preparation of a manuscript requires expert care. I have had the good fortune to work with Bette Keith and Marjorie Quick, who typed the manuscript, and Ginie Reynolds, Vonnie Vaughn, and Christine Kamping, who word-processed the many versions.

My very special gratitude goes to the Russell Sage Foundation where I was a Visiting Fellow during the academic year 1982–1983. While this book was going through the many phases of production, I had the opportunity to concentrate fully on my next research project unencumbered by other academic obligations. It is my pleasure to thank Marshall Robinson, Peter de Janosi, and Alida Brill for their continued interest and support.

All these people share in the success of this book; whatever errors of fact or judgment remain are mine.

1. Child Abuse as a Social Problem

The date was March 26, 1973. The weather in Washington, D.C., was rainy and mild. On this typical early spring day a very atypical event was under way. Senator Walter F. Mondale (D., Minn.), an erstwhile presidential candidate, was holding the first day of hearings on his Child Abuse Prevention Act. Never before had Congress demonstrated so great a concern for child abuse. These hearings were proof to all who were interested that child abuse was firmly established on the congressional agenda. The hearings began at 9:30 A.M. in the wood-paneled offices of the Dirksen Building. Second among the witnesses, and the most riveting, was "Jolly K.," founder of Parents Anonymous. Mondale asked her if she had abused her child:

> "Yes, I did, to the point of almost causing death several times. . . . It was extreme serious physical abuse. . . . Once I threw a rather large kitchen knife at her and another time I strangled her because she lied to me. . . . This was up to when she was 6½ years old. . . . It was ongoing. It was continuous.
> "I had gone to 10 county and State facilities. Out of those, all but one were very realistic places to turn to. Six of them were social services, protective service units. . . . Even the most ignorant listeners could have picked up what I was saying, that I was abusing [my daughter], and that I was directly asking for mental health services. . . . I wanted to keep my child. I wanted to get rid of my problem. She wasn't the problem. She was the recipient of my behavior."

Senator Jennings Randolph (D., W. Va.) turned the questioning to Jolly K.'s experience with Parents Anonymous, the self-help group for abusive parents styled after Alcoholics Anonymous (AA). Like AA, Parents Anonymous encourages abusive parents to talk about their fears and frustrations with child rearing, and their guilt and anguish over the harm members have caused their children. Randolph went straight to the political heart of the matter, asking how successful Parents Anonymous was in eliminating further abuse and keeping children at home. Happily, Randolph learned of the program's success:

> "Most of them have the children in the home. Most of them have the symptomatic behavior of abuse now removed. . . .
> "We encourage parents to utilize us until they feel comfortable enough to go out and utilize other existing services. . . . where they can work more deeply with internal problems.[2]

Jolly K. was the perfect witness, cutting through academic pieties to convince the assembled senators, witnesses, and journalists of the gravity of the problem. She was, figuratively, a sinner who had repented and been saved by her own hard work and the loving counsel of her friends. But more importantly, she embodied the American conception of a social problem: individually rooted, described as an illness, and solvable by occasional doses of therapeutic conversation.

Senator Mondale encouraged this conventional understanding of the problem. Any more elaborate view, especially one which focused on injustice as a source of social problems, threatened to scuttle his efforts to move this small piece of categorical legislation through Congress. With able maneuvering, Mondale's approach prevailed, and on January 31, 1974, President Richard M. Nixon signed the Child Abuse Prevention and Treatment Act (CAPTA) into law. The legislation authorized $86 million to be spent over the next three and a half years, mostly on research and demonstration projects, though some funds were earmarked for discretionary social service grants to the states.[3]

Eighty-six million dollars for child abuse, a problem which did not even warrant an entry in the *Readers' Guide to Periodical Literature* until 1968![4] How did this happen? Or, asked more elaborately, how did child abuse, a small, private-sector charity concern, become a multimillion-dollar public social welfare issue? This book tries to provide an answer. It is a study of the politics of child abuse and neglect, a history and analysis of political issue creation and agenda setting.

The book has three broad aims. *The first aim is, of course, to recount the history of child abuse policy-making over the last three decades.* The story begins in 1955 with the renewed efforts of the American Humane Association (AHA), a charitable organization engaged in research on child and animal maltreatment, to ascertain the extent of physical child abuse and the adequacy of governmental response. The AHA shared its findings with the U.S. Children's Bureau, which in 1963 proposed a model statute to encourage reporting of physical child abuse. Other organizations as diverse as the American Academy of Pediatrics and the Council of State Legislatures proposed different model reporting laws. Bombarded with model statutes and facing no opposition, state legislatures passed child abuse reporting laws with dizzying speed. The demand for services, or at least the demand for workable service models, encouraged Mondale to sponsor federal legislation in 1973; legislation which was successful despite opposition from the Nixon administration. That legislation appeared to be untouchable until President Ronald Reagan was elected and stripped social programs bare in an attempt to balance the budget and shift the initiative for solving social problems to the private sector.

But the history of child abuse policy making is also a vehicle for the discussion of political agenda setting more generally, this book's second aim. E. E. Schattschneider, the dean of agenda-setting studies by virtue of his classic work *The Semi-Sovereign People,* asserted that the most important decisions made in any polity were those determining which issues would become part of public discourse. "Some issues are organized into politics while others are organized out," Schattschneider said with economy.[5] This book tries to elaborate the process by which issues get "organized into politics." It is an attempt to advance our understanding of the first step of the policy process, the step where those issues which *will* receive governmental attention are chosen from among those issues which *could* receive governmental attention.

The third aim of the book is to discuss what I call "the public use of private deviance." My interest here is to link child abuse with other issues dealing with violence and personal autonomy (e.g., rape, domestic violence, incest, sexual abuse, and attacks on the elderly) which have recently become part of the governmental agenda. Like child abuse, each of these issues was accepted as a proper concern of government in part because it was represented as deviance improperly protected by the privacy of the family. But the focus on deviance—and medical deviance at that—turned policy makers away from considering the social-structural and social-psychological underpinnings of abuse and neglect. The advantages and limitations of the deviance approach, which are essentially the advantages and limitations of liberal reform, constitute the third theme.

The book focuses on decision making in governmental organizations. I am most interested in the process whereby public officials learn about new problems, decide to give them their personal attention, and mobilize their organizations to respond to them. Of course, this process is influenced by the type of problems considered and the organizational and political milieux in which officials work. Thus the book will give particular attention to the fact that during the agenda-setting process child abuse was vigorously portrayed as a noncontroversial issue. Disagreements about how best to respond to abuse were suppressed, along with the great debate over the extent to which government ought properly to intervene in family matters. These conflicts became much more apparent as the political climate grew more conservative in the late 1970s and early 1980s. Indeed, government's attention to child abuse in the post World War II period must be understood as part of a larger concern with equity and social justice. So too the movement away from governmental responsibility for child protection should be viewed as part of a larger concern with governmental efficiency and traditional patterns of family authority.

The book is organized chronologically, presenting three case studies of agenda setting in governmental institutions, and an analysis of the role of the mass and professional media. Chapter 2 discusses the theoretical approaches to agenda setting, expanding and linking the organizational, interest group, and economic literature. Chapter 3 shows how the first contemporary governmental interest in child abuse arose through communication between the American Humane Association and the U.S. Children's Bureau. Chapter 4 makes the connection between governmental response to child abuse and popular awareness of the problem, and illuminates the varying roles played by the professional and mass media in making the public aware of child abuse. Chapter 5 presents the states' response to child abuse. Here we shall discuss the rapid adoption of child abuse reporting laws—all fifty states passed legislation in only five years—as well as present a case study of the passage of New Jersey's first reporting law. Chapter 6 considers how Congress became aware of popular and professional interest in abuse and chose to do something about it. Chapter 7, the last chapter, reviews the findings about agenda setting and concludes with an assessment of the future of the public use of private deviance. The remainder of this chapter sets the stage by defining social problems, discussing the invention of child abuse as a social problem, presenting the difficulties in defining and measuring abuse, and elaborating on the theme of the public use of private deviance.

The Invention of Child Abuse

Defining Social Problems

Examples of the brutal or neglectful treatment of children are found as far back as records have been kept. But the mere existence of a condition like cruelty to children does not mean that every society which witnessed abuse condemned it, although some individuals may have.[6] A social problem goes beyond what a few, or even many, individuals feel privately: a social problem is a social construct. Its "creation" requires not only that a number of individuals feel a conflict of value over what is and what ought to be, but also that individuals organize to change the condition, and achieve at least a modicum of recognition for their efforts from the wider public.[7]

The social problem we know as child abuse is a product of America's Gilded Era. Until the 1870s maltreatment of white children was not a part of public debate. Extreme brutality was handled by the court on a case-by-case basis. Less severe cases may have upset the neighbors, but child-rearing decisions were considered the prerogative of parents, particularly fathers.

What happened, then, to make the public think of abuse as a social problem? The answer rests in part with the "Mary Ellen" case, a rather grisly instance of abuse which received widespread publicity in New York City in 1874. A "friendly visitor" discovered that the girl had regularly been bound and beaten by her stepmother. Outrage over the incident precipitated the forming of the New York Society for the Prevention of Cruelty to Children, the first child protection association in the country.

A single incident, however momentous, does not guarantee that concerned individuals will view the event as an example of a larger problem, and organize to solve it. To bring a problem to light requires leadership to create the groups necessary to act, and a cultural willingness to accept the problem as defined. Sociologist Neil Smelser calls this latter requirement "structural readiness for change."[8] The requirement of structural readiness does not mean, of course, that if certain conditions are not defined as problems the time is simply not right for recognition. Repression keeps certain conditions from being defined as problems. Nonetheless, the creation of a social problem does require some public receptivity.[9]

The ideal of a "protected childhood" provided the cultural backdrop necessary for the acceptance of abuse as a social problem. Cruelty to children, especially by parents, appeared much more troublesome when contrasted with the "modern" image of childhood as a safe and sheltered period of life. Scholars have offered a number of rather different explanations for the creation of the modern family and its reverence for childhood.[10] Phillipe Ariès suggests that the transformation of formal education under the Scholastics, the idea of privacy, and the rise of a partly urban, commercial society, conjoined to initiate the affective family and attention to childhood as a separate time of life deserving of protection. Lawrence Stone proposes another explanation. The rise of "affective individualism" in the West produced a bourgeois family based on friendship and sentiment. Both Ariès and Stone locate the origins of the modern family in the bourgeoisie. In contrast, Edward Shorter locates the origin of the modern family in changes in village culture. Technological innovations which allowed capital surplus freed villagers from patriarchal village mores and permitted the development of "familial empathy."

Though they disagree on many points, these explanations all concur with the idea that in the modern family, normal, correct child rearing excludes excessive violence or gross inattention. In America, belief in a protected childhood was the product of three forces—natural rights ideology, commitment to civic education, and the increasing number of bourgeois families—which converged in the post–Civil War period. During Radical Reconstruction natural rights ideology, with its commitment to equality, drew a growing number of supporters. Its rhetoric frequently extended natural rights to animals and children. Elbridge T. Gerry, one of the founders of the New York Society for the Prevention of Cruelty to Children, was an advocate of this position. In 1882 he wrote that "at the present day in this country, children have *some* rights, which even parents are bound to respect," sentiments much less evident a century earlier.[11]

Those who might not fully support the notion of the natural rights of children could still see the wisdom of educating children for citizenship. Indeed, America's experiment in republican government produced a long-standing commitment to civic education.[12] But after the Civil War the support for civic education in part superceded older, more traditional educational concerns. Childhood was no longer seen only as the time to form a moral adult, but also the time to forge a separate citizen of the republic. Historian Stanley N. Katz nicely summarizes this transformation:

> Philip Greven has graphically described how evangelical
> and even moderate colonial Americans self-consciously set
> out to subdue their children's independence and to make
> them conform to the dictates of divine law and parental wis-

dom. So long as salvation was generally perceived as dependent upon conversion, it was obviously the parents' highest duty so to treat their children. For the Rousseauian modern parent, however, precisely the opposite was indicated. For them the child was a fragile flower to be cultivated, nourished and appreciated so that its finest qualities could realize their potential. The discovery of childhood and an optimistic view of child psychology thus transformed child-parent relations.[13]

The increasing number of bourgeois families, where the wife and children did not work for wages, gave substance to this view. A protected childhood became a standard by which well-to-do families could measure the social adequacy and integration of less fortunate families. Well-to-do activists, who could afford to provide such protection for their children, organized child protective societies beginning in the 1870s. But as we shall see later, they were immediately confronted by the unsettling observation that economic conditions constrained many parents from providing such protection for their children.

The Mary Ellen Case

The first child protection society was formed in 1874 in response to the notorious Mary Ellen Wilson case. Mary Ellen's plight was crushingly Victorian. She lived in the home of Francis and Mary Connolly, but she was not the blood relative of either, being the illegitimate daughter of Mrs. Connolly's first husband, Thomas McCormack, and Fanny Wilson.[14] A neighbor noticed that Mrs. Connolly treated the child brutally, beating her with a leather thong and allowing her to go ill-clothed in bad weather. The neighbor told Mrs. Etta Angell Wheeler, a "friendly visitor," who then went to Henry Bergh, the founder of the American Society for the Prevention of Cruelty to Animals (ASPCA) to ask if the ASPCA could help the child.[15]

The popular version of Bergh's response reports that Bergh successfully argued in court that Mary Ellen ought to be removed from her cruel guardians because she, as a member of the animal kingdom, deserved the same protection as abused animals. Actually, the case was argued by Bergh's friend and counsel, Elbridge T. Gerry, who had Mary Ellen removed from her unwholesome surroundings by a petition for a writ *de homine replegando*, an old English writ for removing a person from the custody of another. The case was a staple in New York newspapers for months, no doubt aided by the fact that Mrs. Wheeler's husband was a journalist. In December 1874 the New York Society for the Prevention of Cruelty to Children (New York SPCC) was formed, with Gerry, who had successfully removed Mary Ellen from her home and won a prison sentence for her stepmother, as the moving force.[16]

Gerry and his friends had a ready model for action when the Mary Ellen case came to their attention: the British and American animal protection societies. Animal protection societies were first formed in England in 1824. Henry Bergh, who founded the American SPCA in 1866, explicitly used the Royal British SPCA as his guide. When not ignored, both the English and American SPCAs were the objects of laughter and scorn. Only the meat-packing industry, whose unsanitary and cruel practices were often attacked, ever paid them much attention. Indeed, the important role of the animal protective societies in promoting sanitary meat and milk processing has largely been forgotten today, when we remember the SPCAs only as the perfect example of frivolous Victorian do-gooding.

In 1870, at Bergh's invitation, Gerry became counsel for the ASPCA. Though fourteen years separated them, Bergh and Gerry had similar careers. Both came from prominent Protestant families which provided them with private incomes, both attended Columbia University, both practiced law, and both were devoted to a vision of rational Christian social improvement. Their friends and acquaintances included the political and social leaders of New York City and State. It is no wonder, then, that when Mary Ellen's plight became known to them, one of their responses was to call a meeting.

The Rise of Protective Societies

The objective of the New York SPCC was to rescue children from situations which imperiled their morals, safety, health, or welfare—pretty much in that order. The New York Society's emphasis was on child rescue rather than family rehabilitation. It created for itself a police and placement function whereby it identified and prosecuted abusers, referring the children it "saved" to large child-minding institutions. It is often assumed that the New York SPCC usurped the policelike powers it wielded, but this is completely untrue. Rather, the cruelty and neglect statute passed by the New York legislature in 1881 at the Society's request made it a misdemeanor to interfere with the work of designated child protection agents. As a consequence the Society had enormous power over the poor families it monitored, even if it did help many children out of dangerous situations.

The New York SPCC's emphasis on controlling the poor is perhaps best portrayed by the engravings (and later photographs) depicting children "before" and "after" the Society's intervention. The *Annual Report* of 1876 shows two engravings of Ellen Conners. In the "before" picture, the child is portrayed as wild, ragged, badly cut about the face, and rather suspiciously scratching her genitals. In the "after" picture, Ellen is sweetly dressed in layer upon layer of fashionable clothes, and her hands, far from being anywhere near her crotch, are decorously hidden in a rabbit-fur muff. The emphasis on personal control in the engraving reflects the social goals of the organization: "These little waifs of society were destined to become the fathers and mothers of this Republic. If they were neglected the permanent interest of the Republic would be neglected."[17]

Not all SPCCs ran on the child rescue model favored by the New York Society. The Philadelphia and Illinois (Chicago) SPCCs responded more to problems of drunkenness, desertion, or neglect than to physical abuse of children. These SPCCs (as well as the New York Society) ran temporary shelters where women and children could find a brief respite from violence or economic distress.[18] The Massachusetts (Boston) SPCC was among the first of the protective societies to emphasize "family rehabilitation." Its members worked to bring about the social, political, and economic changes necessary to relieve "destitution." The child rescue and family rehabilitation approaches were at war for almost forty years. The old-line Scientific Charity advocates favored child rescue, which often separated parents and children. The Progressives, on the other hand, promoted the family rehabilitation view, which kept the child at home or in a homelike setting.

The Decline of Protective Societies

The family rehabilitation approach ultimately won. Many reasons are offered for its victory, most centering on the philosophical tenets of the Progressives. The Progressives, with their commitment to childhood as a stage of physical and civic development, felt that normal childhood was childhood in a home and thus the breakup of the family was not favored. To implement their beliefs, the Progressives encouraged the creation of a familylike setting in the juvenile courts and argued that the state had a positive duty to protect women and children. Progressives dismantled the poorhouse, fought against child labor, and encouraged mothers' pensions.

The power of the family-centered response to child welfare was best demonstrated at the first White House Conference on Dependent Children in 1909, whose report stated unequivocally that

> home life is the highest and finest product of civilization. It is the great molding force of mind and of character. Children should not be deprived of it except for urgent and compelling reasons. Children of parents of worthy character, suffering from temporary misfortune and children of reasonably efficient and deserving mothers who are without the support of the normal breadwinner, should, as a rule, be kept with their parents, such aid being given as may be necessary to maintain suitable homes for the rearing of the children.[19]

The Conference also supported the establishment of a federal Children's Bureau, a proposal first introduced in Congress in 1906. The Progressives further urged that child protection become a responsibility of public child welfare departments, and in this they were often supported by socially minded SPCCs like the Massachusetts Society.[20] In 1923, C. C. Carstens, once the secretary of the Massachusetts SPCC and later director of the Child Welfare League of America, wrote that only half of the more than 800 humane societies formed since 1874 had survived, and many of them were only limping along.[21]

But the decline of SPCCs and the eclipse of cruelty as a separate problem of child welfare can be explained by the operation of large institutions as much as by the philosophical beliefs of the Progressives. These organizational reasons have gone largely unnoticed until now. The child rescue approach was made possible by the previous existence of large, asylumlike institutions which would accept the rescued child. But in the 1870s and 1880s the "placing out" system (i.e., foster care), which assigned children to willing and interested families, began competing with orphanages.

The increasing popularity of the "placing out" method had enormous consequences for the SPCCs, whose special function originally had been to identify and refer children. When one more child was added to an orphanage, the personality or characteristics of that child were not terribly important to the functioning of the institution. To say the least, institutional care in the late nineteenth century did not promote individualism among children. But when a child was referred for placing out, the characteristics of the child were very important. The family which took the child had to deal with him or her as an individual. "Placing out" agencies thus wanted desperately to control the composition of their clientele.

As public agencies began taking over such functions, they too wanted to do their own casefinding. Programmatic success required that public child welfare agencies pick which clients they would serve. In this light the reasons for the decline of SPCCs become clearer. For organizational as well as philosophical reasons, other agencies were opposed to the SPCCs' avowed function of casefinding. Only in places like New York City, with its firmly entrenched child-minding institutions, did the traditional SPCCs survive. Elsewhere their work was incorporated into public child welfare agencies.

The longevity of the New York SPCC was also aided by a well-established contract system which dispensed public money to private institutions for the care of poor, abused, neglected, or wayward children. Homer Folks estimated that in 1890 the New York SPCC "practically controlled the lives of an average number of about fifteen thousand children, and an average annual expenditure for their support of more than one and one half million dollars. Its influence has done more to strengthen and perpetuate the subsidy or contract system, as it existed prior to 1894, than any other one factor."[22] The large institutions and the New York SPCC formed a partnership wherein the SPCC found children, the orphanages provided the care, and the state supplied a constant stream of funds. Opposition to this arrangement came from the fact that it encouraged institutional care, not that it lacked accountability for the spending of public monies. The potential exploitation of a per capita billing system went largely unrecognized. The main management problem, as seen by Josephine Shaw Lowell, was access by the State Board of Charities for inspection of the institutions for health code violations.[23]

The experience of the New York SPCC was unusual, however, and even its power declined with the Great Depression. By World War II, the SPCC movement was completely enervated nationwide. The pressing needs of children displaced by war drove protective work even further into the social services backwater.

The Rediscovery of Child Abuse

By the 1950s, public interest in abuse and neglect was practically nonexistent, and even social workers did not rate it highly as a professional concern. How were these issues rediscovered and ultimately adopted as problems which government should help to solve? The specific answers to these questions need to be understood in their historical context.

The rediscovery of child abuse occurred in an era when issues of equity and social responsibility dominated public discourse. A long period of concern with a variety of equity issues began with the civil rights movement in the mid and late 1950s. The 1962 amendments to the Social Security Act urging child welfare services in every county demonstrated that the interests of children were part of the equity cycle. The child welfare amendments were followed by the "War on Poverty," which emphasized the importance of services to children as a method of eliminating poverty. In 1967 the equity cycle was given tremendous impetus by the Supreme Court's *In re Gault* opinion, which extended Bill of Rights protection to children. Later, the months spent crafting the Comprehensive Child Development Act (ultimately vetoed by President Nixon) educated members of Congress to the centrality (and difficulty) of providing adequately for the needs of all children.

Not unimportantly, this equity cycle coincided with years of great economic prosperity. Real GNP doubled between 1950 and 1970. Consequently, the material gains of one group did not appear to threaten the gains of others. It was a time when politics seemed to exist without trade-offs.

The concern for children was not limited to government. Pediatricians, the most prestigious group dealing with youngsters, enjoyed two decades of notable success in conquering deadly childhood diseases. With the ability to cure or prevent many children's diseases, pediatricians had the status, skills, and the slack resources to invest in research on problems which were at least partly behavioral in origin.

But it was the work of radiologists like John Caffey, P. V. Woolley, and W. A. Evans which alerted pediatricians to the specific problem of abuse. In 1946 Caffey first reported a number of cases in which infants had multiple long bone fractures and subdural hematomas. He did not, however, speculate on the causes of trauma. In 1953, Woolley and Evans suggested that similar injuries might be caused by the children's caretakers. In 1957, Caffey reexamined his original data and concluded that the trauma might well have been willfully perpetrated by parents. It took almost a decade for physicians to conclude that some parents were violently assaulting their children, a delay caused by professional cautiousness and a profound psychological resistance to recognizing that some parental behavior departed so radically from the ideal.[24]

This research, as well as the early work done by social workers,[25] was well known to pediatricians like C. Henry Kempe and his colleagues, who were investigating the causes as well as the appropriate responses to physical abuse. In 1962 they published their famous article "The Battered-Child Syndrome" in the prestigious *Journal of the American Medical Association.*[26] Within weeks of its publication, stories on child abuse were featured in popular magazines like *Time* and the *Saturday Evening Post.* The publication of the Kempe article is often used to date the rediscovery of child abuse as a social problem. But in point of fact, the popular articles based on Kempe's research were equally important in creating the sense of an urgent national problem.

Defining and Measuring Child Abuse and Neglect

Problems of Definition

The first people to identify a problem often shape how others will perceive it. Nowhere is this truer than with the issue of child abuse. In "The Battered-Child Syndrome" Kempe and his associates define the problem as "a clinical condition in young children who received serious physical abuse, generally from a parent or foster parent."[27] Based on a survey of the literature and an examination of 302 cases reported in 71 hospitals, the authors suggested that abusers had serious psychological problems but were not psychopaths:

> Psychiatric factors are probably of prime importance in the pathogenesis of the disorder, but our knowledge of these factors is limited. Parents who inflict abuse on their children do not necessarily have psychopathic or sociopathic personalities or come from borderline socioeconomic groups, although most published cases have been in these categories. *In most cases some defect of character structure is probably present; often parents may be repeating the type of child care practiced on them.*[28]

The individually centered psychological construction of the problem made it seem very self-contained. Governmental response to a self-contained, serious, but noncontroversial issue ought to be easy to obtain. And easy it was. Once alerted to the problem, the U.S. Children's Bureau and other organizations drafted model child abuse reporting laws which were rapidly passed by all state legislatures. The speed of adoption rested largely on this narrow construction of the problem. The early California reporting statute reflected this view. Child abuse was defined as "physical injuries or injury which appear to have been inflicted upon [the child] by other than accidental means."[29]

Almost as quickly as this narrow view took substance in the law, it was replaced by a more comprehensive construction of the problem. As scholars in a number of fields examined the problem, the socioeconomic considerations of child abuse—its connection to joblessness, inadequate housing, and other chronic social ills—became evident and popular. (Interestingly, gender and power considerations were absent from most of this analysis.) In 1974, the federal Child Abuse Prevention and Treatment Act (CAPTA) incorporated a fairly comprehensive definition of the problem. CAPTA defines child abuse and neglect together:

> "Child Abuse and Neglect" means the physical or mental injury, sexual abuse, negligent treatment, or maltreatment of any child under the age of eighteen by a person who is responsible for the child's welfare under circumstances which indicate the child's health or welfare is harmed or threatened thereby.[30]   — CAPTA

The definition of child abuse found in CAPTA provides a more comprehensive statement of the problem than one might expect after reading the transcripts of the legislative hearings. In the public debate over the congressional legislation, comprehensive definitions were actively suppressed in order to enhance the noncontroversial nature of the issue.

In fact, at each point when child abuse achieved a governmental agenda, the narrow definition was emphasized. The narrow definition predominated during agenda setting for three related reasons. First, agenda setting by the Children's Bureau and state legislatures occurred while the narrow definition was still quite popular. Second, physicians preferred the narrow definition because it best fit their experiences in hospital emergency rooms, and physicians, by virtue of their high status, had easy and early access to officials. Third and most important, a narrow definition of abuse reduced conflict, particularly from right-wing critics. The use of a narrow definition thwarted a potential conservative challenge to what might be seen as governmental action against normal parental discipline.

Favoring the narrow definition during agenda setting had important, long-lasting effects on the shape of child abuse policy. By ignoring neglect, the connection between poverty and maltreatment was purposely blurred. In fact, strenuous efforts were made to popularize abuse as a problem knowing no barriers of class, race, or culture. For some politicians, particularly Mondale, this was part of a conscious strategy to dissociate efforts against abuse from unpopular poverty programs. The purpose was to describe abuse as an all-American affliction, not one found solely among low-income people. While acknowledging that abuse and neglect were found in all strata of society, a number of scholars severely criticized this approach and maintained that the larger number of cases found among the poor was not only a function of reporting biases, but was present because poor people actually abused or neglected their children more. The message of the research was not that poor people were bad people or bad parents, but that the deprivations of poverty were real and encouraged abuse. These findings were very unpopular, however, and the "myth of classlessness" promoted during agenda setting was very difficult to counter.[31]

Measuring Child Abuse

No one actually knows the extent of child abuse and neglect, or whether their incidence is increasing or decreasing. At the National Conference for Family Violence Researchers, Professor Richard Gelles summed up the difficulties in measuring abuse and neglect: "We don't know a *damn* thing about whether child abuse is increasing, decreasing or staying the same."[32] It is not merely the lack of a commonly agreed-upon definition which hinders counting but also problems of methodology—of criteria, applications, and evidence—which make the task so difficult. Not surprisingly, the numbers vary widely. One of the lowest estimates comes from a *Pediatric News* (1975) report suggesting that one child dies of abuse every day, yielding a yearly incidence of 365 deaths. Using national survey data, David Gil (1970) offers a much higher figure, but for a different phenomenon. Gil suggests that for the year ending in October 1965, between 2.53 and 4.07 million American adults *knew* of physically abusive families, figures which Richard Light (1974) statistically adjusted to reach his estimate of approximately 500,000 cases of physical abuse during the year under study.[33]

From a public policy perspective, two estimates have been more important than all the others: one "guess" in an early medical article and the official reporting statistics gathered over the last several years. In fact, this early medical "guess" did not even mention statistics. Instead child abuse was described as possibly more life-threatening than a host of well-known and feared childhood diseases. The story of this nonnumerical estimate bears telling because it shows how powerful a credible source can be in defining the extent of a social problem, even when that source offers no figures whatsoever.

In 1962, Dr. C. Henry Kempe and his associates published their famous article "The Battered-Child Syndrome" in the *Journal of the American Medical Association*.[34] In an accompanying editorial, the country's most powerful arbiters of medical knowledge wrote that "it is likely that [the battered child syndrome] will be found to be a more frequent cause of death than such well recognized and thoroughly studied diseases as leukemia, cystic fibrosis, and muscular dystrophy."[35] The editors were merely speculating about the extent of abuse and qualified all their comparisons. Politicians and journalists were not always as careful. Official after official and article after article repeated the comparison as though it were fact.

The consistency with which the AMA *Journal*'s editorial was cited was probably more important than its accuracy. Gilbert Y. Steiner suggests that where estimates of problem size differ substantially, it is difficult to establish the legitimacy of the problem. He noted that the differing estimates of the size of the problem of domestic violence (ranging from 7.5 million to 526,000 episodes a year) allowed detractors to chip away at congressional support.[36] Modest and consistent estimates seem to inspire the most confidence, especially in cases of the public response to private deviance. Deviance can only exist as such if there is not too much of it.

The official reporting statistics, the second important measure of child abuse, do not indicate a modest problem at all. In 1979, the Child Protection Division of the American Humane Association compiled all the official abuse and neglect reports made in the fifty states and the territories. Nationwide there were 711,142 official reports of maltreatment, but the type of maltreatment could only be discerned in 234,000 of the reports. Of these, 25.1% were designated solely as abuse. Of course, there is a certain amount of comparing apples and oranges in the compilation of these figures. No uniform legal definition exists, and case-counting procedures differ markedly from state to state. Nonetheless, these figures give us some sense of the magnitude of the problem as understood by officials, regardless of how many or what kind of cases are not reported.[37]

These official figures have been used to promote and maintain interest in the problem. Similar figures were paraded during the first CAPTA reauthorization hearings in 1977 and again in 1981 to show the magnitude of the problem. These numbers are susceptible to political manipulation in an era of social service cutbacks. If reporting is lax and service positions go unstaffed, the number of cases will eventually fall off as concerned individuals concede the futility of reporting. If the numbers decline, then the problem can be described as waning, perhaps even as disappearing because of the application of a measured dose of governmental intervention. Lower numbers, in turn, can be used to justify lower expenditures, in a widening circle of verbal deceit and programmatic despair.

The Public Use of Private Deviance

Neglect and abuse are so common that it ought to be hard to maintain the image that they are rare, deviant behaviors. But the construction of this problem as one of medical deviance has proven extraordinarily durable. Because physicians played such a large role in setting governmental and media agendas, the first public presentation of the problem was as a social illness.[38] The considerations of power politics are rarely added to the discussion, perhaps because "power" is a public word and "child abuse" is understood to be a private problem.

Many behaviors with significantly aggressive or violent components have been similarly "medicalized." In addition to child abuse, examples include alcoholism, drug abuse, hyperkinesis, and to a lesser degree rape and domestic violence.[39] Earlier in this century alcoholism was variously considered a sin, a crime, or a labor discipline problem, but now it is most often described as a disease. Similar transformations have overtaken drug abuse and hyperkinesis. Rape and domestic violence have been more resistant to this reconstruction, however. Their obvious power connotations limit the applicability of medical metaphors, and thus limit the likelihood of government's adopting the issues. This is not to say that governmental action is necessarily the best way to respond to rape and domestic violence. Instead, the point is that government more readily adopts issues which are constructed as social illness than issues which confront long-established power arrangements.

There are two explanations of the trend toward constructing social problems concerning aggression and violence in terms of medical deviance. The first reason—little discussed in the social policy literature—is that one model of conventional illnesses is constructed on statistical deviation from population norms. In describing this approach to illness David Mechanic writes:

> Doctors frequently can recognize disease because it becomes apparent that in various ways the patient deviates from 'normal values.' In many cases the range of normal values has been established through observations of community populations over a period of time and thus marked deviations can easily be determined.[40]

In the case of behaviors rather than physical functioning, it is quite easy to assert that particular actions diverge from the measured—or even assumed—norm. With the rise of the concept of mental illness in this century, practically any disvalued behavior can be defined as medical deviance. In fact, merely by its being statistically rare a behavior can become disvalued and subject to medical response.[41]

The second reason for constructing some problems in terms of medical deviance is that medicine offers solutions to these problems, solutions which in the short run appear to be—and often are—humane and caring. Medicine professes to have solutions—ranging from psychotropic drugs, to therapy, to the mental hospital—which are supposed to treat rather than punish the sick person. Medical solutions both maintain and promote the power of medicine and medical professionals while simultaneously reassuring us that we live in a humanitarian rather than a punitive or repressive society.[42]

The political advantages of the construction of social problems as medical deviance are easy to see. Medicine views illness as individual in location if not cause, so a medical construction is consonant with the American individualistic approach to solving problems. By defining problems in terms of medical deviance, the status quo is maintained, at least in the short run.

The political limitations of the medical deviance approach are also obvious. Individualizing problems turns policy makers away from considering their structural causes. Policies which "treat" medical deviance no doubt help thousands of people, but they do so at the cost of expanding state intervention without increasing the state's ability to redress the fundamental inequities which underlie, say, abuse and neglect. Conservative critics then bemoan the loss of family autonomy and liberal critics bemoan the band-aid quality of public efforts, particularly the fact that public monies are not targeted where the problem is most severe and pressing. Socialist critics add that individually centered responses to social problems are designed to maintain existing power relations.

The people who promoted governmental interest in child abuse were mostly social welfare liberals, although the construction of the problem encouraged support across the political spectrum. They saw child abuse as a public health matter, with implications much like those of venereal disease. The case for state action was made on the grounds that child abuse was a social illness which had been improperly protected by the private status of the family. The government used the notion of medical deviance as the rationale for intervening in the family—hence the phrase "the public use of private deviance." At the same time government reaffirmed the essential split between the public and private spheres. Theorists like Zillah Eisenstein suggest that such actions eventually destabilize the liberal state and work to break down the public-private distinction which such policies intend to uphold.[43] The bureaucrats and legislators who promoted an interest in child abuse did not take such a long-sighted view, however. They believed that governmental action would aid the afflicted even if only modestly. They gave child abuse their professional attention, and then went about their jobs.

2. Theoretical Approaches to Agenda Setting

Defining Agenda Setting

In political science, a great deal of attention is given to *how* political problems are resolved, but very much less attention is paid to *which* problems actually enter the public domain.[1] This process is called agenda setting and is defined as the course by which issues are adopted for public consideration and, perhaps, remedy. Here I am particularly interested in how public officials learn about new problems, decide to give them their personal attention, and mobilize their organizations to respond to them. Interest in agenda setting per se is not much more than a decade old. It emerges from the great elitism-pluralism debates of the postwar period which focused attention on which people—and which preferences—were to be heard in a democracy and with what results.[2]

In their pioneering work, Roger W. Cobb and Charles D. Elder distinguish between the systemic and the formal agenda. "The systemic agenda," they wrote, "consists of all issues that are commonly perceived by members of the political community as meriting public attention and as involving matters within the legitimate jurisdiction of existing governmental authority." The formal agenda has a much narrower institutional focus, being defined as "that set of items explicitly up for the active and serious consideration of authoritative decision-makers."[3]

The distinction Cobb and Elder present is essential, and it is perserved in this study, but with somewhat different terminology and more gradations. Instead of the term "formal agenda" I employ "governmental agenda" or "public agenda" when discussing those matters being considered by governmental institutions. Similarly I do not use the term "systemic agenda," instead substituting two other expressions. The term "popular agenda" is employed to designate awareness on the part of the mass public, and "professional agenda" is used to designate awareness among those members of the public informed about a given issue who may promote a particular expert view of a problem.

The distinction between popular and professional agendas proves very useful. An undifferentiated concept of the systemic agenda presents a rather knotty problem, especially if it is seen as "involving matters within the legitimate jurisdiction of existing governmental authority." Determining what is "legitimately" public is precisely the question posed by agenda setting, and many issues achieve a governmental agenda without popular legitimacy, as Cobb, Keith-Ross, and Ross have noted elsewhere.[4]

It is obvious from the terminology that there are many governmental agendas, the result of a large federal system with well-delineated separation of powers. The decentralized nature of American politics is reflected in the research on agenda setting. Until recently, the literature has been dominated by case studies focusing on how one issue has achieved one agenda. With the exception of Nelson Polsby's *Political Innovation In America: The Politics of Policy Initiation*, very little work has compared agenda setting on a variety of issues.[5] Similarly, until now there has been almost no research on how the same issue achieves different governmental agendas.

The single-issue focus of most research is not surprising, given the enormous amount of institutional knowledge and substantive research necessary to determine the origins of a particular proposal. The individual case material is more cumulative than it might seem at first glance, however. Within certain policy areas—notably environmental concerns,[6] social problems of the elderly,[7] medicine,[8] and women's issues[9]—there has been a sustained and reflective effort to analyze a variety of policy innovations.

Together the case studies and the conceptual works offer quite different explanations for the expansion and changing composition of governmental agendas. The explanations do not take the form of full-blown theories in either a political science or Newtonian physics sense of the term. Instead, they ought to be thought of as sets of hypotheses emerging from particular schools of thought. Three approaches have emerged, emphasizing respectively organizational behavior; issue careers, cycles, and clusters; and economic growth.

The concerns of each approach are different. The organizational approach focuses on the decisions made by policy makers acting in their official roles. The issue careers and cycles approach focuses on the emergence and definition of a problem, and has its roots in the interest group literature. The economic growth school, particularly public choice theory, does not try to determine which specific issues will be adopted but instead puts forward a general principle of governmental growth (majoritarian voting with logrolling) and its negative consequences (uncontrollable public spending and economic inefficiency).

It might be tempting to call for a grand synthesis of the three theoretical approaches, but the success of such an effort is doubtful. The approaches vary in unit and level of analysis, and perhaps more important, in the values and traditions which motivate inquiry. The variety in the theoretical approaches is an important aspect of the research because it reminds us of the multiplicity of forces—bureaucratic, interest group, and systemic—which impinge on agenda-setting decisions. The more pressing theoretical concern is to provide a clear exposition of the three approaches and elaborate and link them where possible.

Approaches to Agenda Setting

Organizational Approaches and the Stages of Agenda Setting

Practically every aspect of organizational theory has been applied to agenda setting, but the most powerful explanations are derived from the literature on professional career patterns, the influence of professional associations, innovation and the diffusion of innovation, the production behavior of new "firms" (or new governmental offices or voluntary groups), and, recently, the effects of funding sources on the creation of new firms.[10] This literature is rich in hypotheses about what influences agenda setting, but until now has lacked a conceptualization of the agenda setting process itself.

What is needed is a conceptual framework which represents the "natural history" of agenda setting in complex organizations. This approach parallels the method used to examine the life cycle of social problems more generally. Over a decade ago, sociologists Malcolm Spector and John I. Kitsuse wrote that "one task for the sociology of social problems is to search for common elements, stages, or processes among the histories of social problems,—that is to determine if social problems have a 'natural history,' and if so, to describe its stages and the contingencies of its development." They identified one stage of the natural history of social problems as the period when the problem is recognized "by some official organization, agency, or institution of . . . legitimate standing."[11] This book extends this approach to agenda setting itself.

The process of agenda setting can be conceptualized as having four stages: (1) issue *recognition*, (2) issue *adoption*, (3) *setting priorities* among issues, and (4) issue *maintenance*. In stage 1, issue recognition, an official notices a particular problem or concern, and decides that it offers the potential for governmental action. The problem does not have to be newly invented, merely newly discovered by the official.

In stage 2, issue adoption, the official decides whether or not to respond to the problem. It is important to emphasize that the decision to consider an issue is analytically distinct from the decision made between competing policy alternatives. Two conditions must prevail for an issue to be adopted. First, decision makers must share a perception of the legitimacy of governmental responsibility for action on the issue. Second, they must believe that an appropriate response could be found if the issue were to be adopted.

In stage 3, setting priorities among issues, officials reorder the existing agenda to include the new issue. Frequently the setting of priorities involves more than slipping a new issue between two older ones. A new issue may completely dislodge one or more older issues or may cause substantial variations in the depth of consideration the older issues receive.

In stage 4, issue maintenance, the official must move the legislative or administrative process to the point of substantive decision making. We must distinguish between *initial maintenance*, the process whereby an issue first reaches a substantive decision point, and *recurring maintenance*, the process by which established issues are periodically reexamined.[12] Without this long-term maintenance, an issue fails to become an enduring concern of government. This failure is not necessarily regrettable; the governmental agenda would be incredibly crowded if there were no mechanism for removing from public consideration the myriad of horse-and-buggy issues which no longer evoke general interest.

This four-stage conceptualization was employed in the research for this book. But to use these concepts required a very self-conscious effort at translating abstractions into tools. First, it was necessary to construct working definitions of the agenda-setting stages, then to decide what would be considered data, and finally, to examine what triggers the agenda-setting process.

More than anything else, the success of applying the agenda-setting stages in research depends on having detailed information about the institutions under study. Such institutional expertise lets us acknowledge that occasionally the behaviors we examine will span more than one stage. But institutional expertise alone will not insure proper working definitions. Other problems must be overcome. The first is the "asymmetry of proof," or the fact that in agenda-setting research it is easier by far to tell when an issue has achieved the agenda than when it has not.[13] The second problem is the confusion over the proper unit and level of analysis to employ—in other words, does one investigate the actions of people or institutions? A related problem is the linguistic, if not analytical, tendency to personify institutions. And finally there is the "temptation of inevitability," or how the most complex decisions become simple when you know how they turn out.[14]

Once working definitions are constructed, the question of what constitutes "data" remains. The data used in studying agenda setting often consist of small decisions and routine tasks whose products are visible but whose processes leave few traces. Moreover, agenda setting is conventionally thought of as the beginning of the policy process; and the distinctions between agenda setting, the consideration of alternatives, and a substantive, binding decision are often hard to maintain when examining specific cases. In fact, it is not always possible to agree on just what constitutes a case of agenda setting. How do we determine if an issue has ever been addressed by government? If an official has dealt with the issue earlier, deciding at first *not* to act, does a second consideration constitute a new or an old case? The constant redefinition of issues, their waxing and waning, also makes case definition difficult. Such difficulties help to explain why there have been virtually no multi-issue studies of agenda setting.

There is also a fair amount of debate over how the agenda-setting process begins. Admittedly, an official begins the process by recognizing a problem, but what makes him or her notice the problem in the first place? Natural catastrophes or unanticipated human events are usually cited as important triggers of agenda setting, and indeed, a single, serious instance of a problem—a mine disaster or a brutal case of abuse—can instigate governmental action. A catastrophic or unanticipated event is both specific and grave enough to mobilize interest and support. But to focus on catastrophes is to direct research away from the more frequent, but less impressive, origins of agenda setting. Less dramatic inducements include technological and demographic changes and dissatisfaction with the existing distribution of resources.[15] Additionally, there are numerous bureaucratic motivations for issue finding such as career advancement or organizational growth. In organizations, as in society at large, action depends on "structural readiness for change," that elusive but essential combination of political, social, and organizational preparedness which makes the consideration of a problem—but particularly this problem—possible.[16]

Issue Cycles, Careers, and Clusters

By my definition, agenda setting is the process whereby public officials learn about new problems, decide to give them their personal attention, and mobilize their organizations to respond to them. These actions are of course subject to a wide variety of influences. Agenda setting is structured by the type of issue being considered and who supports it, as well as larger socioeconomic forces. A more complete understanding of agenda setting requires us to integrate these concerns with our decision-making approach.

A second approach to agenda setting focuses on social problems themselves rather than on the decision to respond to them. Three types of problem-centered research have been undertaken. The first emphasizes issue cycles, the second emphasizes issue careers, and the third emphasizes issue clusters.

The issue-cycles approach investigates how issues are legitimated to the mass public through the mass media. This approach concentrates on why the media alternately promote and then ignore certain issues. Anthony Downs has argued forcefully that the media portray problems in ways which gloss over fundamental conflicts of value. When such conflicts can no longer be contained the media move on to newer topics. The case study of child abuse coverage in the mass and professional media (presented in chapter 4) allows us to make an important modification in this description: injections of material from professional journals can keep an issue on the agenda of the mass media longer than Downs initially predicted.[17]

The issue-careers approach has a somewhat different emphasis, and focuses not only on the legitimation of issues to the mass public, but also the mobilization of groups and individuals around an issue. According to Roger Cobb and his associates,[18] issues go through four stages: initiation, specification, expansion, and entrance. The specific course an issue takes varies depending on whether important participants are inside or outside government and the extent to which these participants engage the support of the mass public or special interests as well as the support of government.

The recognition that agenda setting varies in consistent ways depending on who participates is an enormously important contribution to systematizing the study of this process. But agenda setting can also vary by type of issue as well as type of participant. The legitimacy of an issue depends as much on how the issue is constructed (i.e., defined and presented) as who participates. In fact, how an issue is defined may largely control who will participate in the decision making.

One of the major concerns of scholars studying the influence of interest groups on legislatures is in developing durable issue categories. The most recent and powerful effort in this vein was made by Michael T. Hayes. Working from a tradition which includes Bauer, Pool and Dexter; Lowi; Froman; Schattschneider; Salisbury; and Heinz; Hayes argues that legislative issues can be categorized by their demand and supply patterns.[19] Within demand patterns he distinguishes between consensual and conflictual inputs, categories analogous to non-zero-sum and zero-sum conflicts. Within supply patterns (or types of legislative response), he distinguishes between no action, delegation (policy without law), and allocation (rule of law). His typology is reproduced in Table 2.1.[20]

Child abuse achieved the agendas of all fifty state legislatures as well as that of Congress. Interestingly, the policies fall into different categories at the state and federal levels. The difference occurs, not surprisingly, because the content of the policy varied at each level. In state legislatures, where policy making first took the form of passing child abuse reporting laws, the issue clearly fits into the "self-regulation" category. Early child abuse reporting laws gave physicians and others the responsibility of reporting suspected abuse, but left the policing of such efforts almost entirely to individual practitioners. As chapter 5 will show, later amendments pushed child abuse laws closer to the regulatory category, where conflicts are "reassigned" to the courts or bureaucracy to be settled on a case-by-case basis.[21]

At the congressional level, it is not quite clear where child abuse fits into this grid. Because it was a highly consensual issue, it seems

TABLE 2.1: TYPOLOGY OF LEGISLATIVE POLICY PROCESSES[a]

	Demand Pattern	
Supply Pattern	Consensual (Non-zero-sum)	Conflictual (Zero-sum)
No bill	Nondecision Barrier 1: community values	Nondecision Barrier 2: institutions and processes
Delegation (policy-without-law)	Self-regulation (legitimized autonomy)	Regulation (extension of group conflict)
Allocation (rule-of-law)	Distribution (pork-barrel politics)	Redistribution (resource transfers)

[a] Michael T. Hayes, *Lobbyists and Legislators: A Theory of Political Markets* (Rutgers University Press, New Brunswick, N.J., 1981), p. 30.

to fit best into the distributional category. But in fact, it is the highly consensual quality of child abuse which gives us pause. The demand pattern for child abuse policy was much more consensual than for any of the issues Hayes considered. He never addressed himself to the possibility that an issue could be truly consensual, i.e., that the issue could have no real opponents, rather than unorganized or uninformed opponents, or opponents mollified by separate legislation.

We need to examine more carefully issues which have such a strong symbolic character. The voting research calls problems like these "valence issues." A valence issue such as child abuse elicits a single, strong, fairly uniform emotional response and does not have an adversarial quality. "Position issues," on the other hand, do not elicit a single response but instead engender alternative and sometimes highly conflictual responses.[22] In Hayes's typology, all issues are implicitly position issues. The difference between consensual and conflictual issues is determined by whether the opposition is organized or not, and whether it is susceptible to disaggregation.

By far the most important attribute of the child abuse issue is its valence quality. Over and over again in interviews with policy makers, child abuse was described as a "motherhood" issue, a somewhat anachronistic designation, considering contemporary conflicts over motherhood. Valence issues have largely been overlooked in agenda-setting research, in part because so much of the research is rooted in the interest group tradition, which stresses the conflictual nature of agenda setting. The search for a place on a governmental agenda is often portrayed as one in which contenders for governmental favors spar with each other in the hallways of power. Unfortunately, this characterization is misleading in many cases of agenda setting in domestic social policy. For these issues agenda setting is often typified by Kotz's discussion on the initiation of the Food Stamp Program, a program which excited much concern and controversy, but which lacked a sharply adversarial tone.[23]

The study of valence issues, especially in public policy making, poses a number of problems. The terms "valence issue" and "position issue" were coined for electoral research. In the past, candidates—particularly presidential candidates—could breeze through their campaigns with a rhetoric that called for nothing more specific than world peace, national strength, or better public education, all of which could be considered valence issues as stated. The luxury of noncontroversial generalities was possible because personal characteristics and party were more important than issue positions in a voter's presidential decision. More recently, however, issues have become increasingly important in presidential voting decisions, and today's voters are more attuned to a candidate's stand on specific policy questions within these larger categories. When examined closely on an issue-by-issue basis, many fewer concerns can properly be categorized as valence issues. It seems clear, then, that two implicit characteristics of electoral valence issues are their *lack of specificity* and their attempt to *reaffirm the ideals of civic life*.

To the extent that a policy issue involves only one widely held ideal (or several complementary ideals) it will be a valence issue. It is important to remember that politicians almost always carry an explicit or implicit solution for any problem they recognize. (The recognition of problems without a plan to remedy them is considered by politicians to be a decidedly academic—and frivolous—enterprise.) Thus, when we speak of a valence policy issue, both the problem and its preferred or intended solutions must invoke a more or less uniform, single-position affirmation of a civic ideal. Of course, the valence-issue/position-issue distinction is best thought of as a continuum. The political culture of America supports a variety of often contradictory ideals, making the unambiguous, uniformly affirmed valence issue relatively rare. Nonetheless, most issues can be categorized as either valence-like or position-like, and child abuse is certainly a valence issue.

One should not assume that because valence issues openly invoke civic ideals that they are necessarily "moral issues." Convention dictates that moral issues include such concerns as prostitution, blue laws, laws regulating the purchase of liquor, race track betting, and the like. These concerns are position issues; no single, unified set of civic values underlies the definition of these problems or their proposed solutions. However, David Mayhew discusses one aspect of moral issues which is relevant to the study of valence issues. Mayhew suggests that for moral issues, constituents often care more about a legislator's stand than the outcome of the legislation. He argues that on moral issues "every member worries about how he should stand and none about which side wins. If each constituency is homogeneous in its views, every member is in a sense a 'winner,' regardless of how close or one-sided the roll calls are."[24] The similarity between moral issues and valence issues is that both demand a public demonstration of political rectitude, where a leader's values are publicly proclaimed.

Clearly, valence issues have an important and largely unrecognized symbolic character. A great deal of attention has been paid to how well political systems absorb and mediate conflicts. Much less attention has been given to the mechanisms for promoting consensus. Valence issues deserve more attention precisely because they constitute one method of encouraging system support, at both the mass and elite levels. Indeed, one may argue that the "democratic revolution" which opened participation in political life to practically every American adult increased the demands, if not the conflict, the political system must absorb. Consequently, processes which encourage system support become more important.

Economic Approaches

Economists who examine agenda setting rarely investigate how one issue or even one type of issue achieves the public agenda. Instead, their interests lie with macroeconomic trends governing the relative size of the public and private sectors of the economy. For instance, public expenditures in America, as measured in constant dollars, rose from 6.8% of the GNP in 1902 to 34.1% in 1970.[25] Economic growth theorists offer several explanations for this phenomenon, variously crediting consumer, producer, and financial forces.[26] Holding center stage in the economic growth school are the public choice theorists who, it is fair to say, look with dismay at the rise in public expenditures. Thomas E. Borcherding, a representative of the public choice approach, has written that "only" about 50% of the growth in public expenditures in this century is a result of changes in relative prices, incomes, population, and their associated interdependencies. Echoing other public choice specialists, Borcherding suggests that the growth in "discretionary" public expenditures results from the success of lobbyists, inefficiencies in public bureaucracy, and increasing sophistication in methods of taxation which hide the true costs of taxes to those who pay them.[27]

Although they focus on the relationship between the size of public budgets and the prospects for economic growth, public choice advocates also provide a political explanation for the growth of government. The public sector expands because of political arrangements allowing majoritarian voting with logrolling (i.e., without cost-benefit constraints).[28] Not only do the budgets of such governments grow by leaps and bounds, but, according to this argument, the whole economy becomes less efficient as a consequence.[29]

Majoritarian voting and logrolling certainly have contributed to the growth of government expenditures and its "penetration" of the private economy. As such, the game-theoretical approach of public choice advocates has been extraordinarily useful in providing a bare-bones description of the consequences of legislative arrangements, thus linking the organizational and economic growth approaches to agenda setting. Legislative arrangements which reward individual officials for discovering new issues may ultimately harm the organization as a whole. From this perspective, the worst decisions legislatures can make are those which initiate or extend policies like AFDC or Medicaid which carry open-ended entitlements. The size of government, its costs, and the efficiency of the economy are all much harder to control when this occurs. Certainly, child abuse policy is not this kind of issue, and the budgetary crises of the 1980s cannot be laid at the door of one categorical social program, or even, most likely, to the sum of them all. Nonetheless, a form of decision making which encourages uncontrolled governmental growth disturbs public choice theorists.[30]

Public choice advocates, however, often wrongly equate the economic inefficiencies of logrolling with civic inefficiencies. They do not sufficiently value the civic benefits of the diversity of interests served by vote trading.[31] Majoritarian voting with logrolling permits some of the needs of those groups formerly un- or underenfranchised to be met when the political climate tolerates new demands. Certainly some considerable fraction of the growth in government spending represents recognition of the newly legitimate demands of the poor, workers, women, and ethnic and racial minorities. Public choice theory turns us away from an important corollary question. Who decides which responsibilities will be met in the public sector, the private sector, or not at all? Danish political scientist Drude Dahlerup suggests an answer: "That the Western political systems do not function the way the pluralists thought, is now a well-established fact. The political system in the Western liberal democracies (and in all other political systems, as well) is biased. Not only do large groups of people never participate in the political process, but issues are also systematically excluded from being seriously considered by the political system. *And the outcome suits the interest of certain groups better than that of others.*"[32] In a socially diverse and economically advanced state, small government favors the already powerful.

In this research, I am most interested in the organizational approach. The focus is on how public officials decide to promote new issues. In the chapters which follow I shall use the conceptual framework of agenda setting in complex organizations to present the natural history of child abuse policy making in the U.S. Children's Bureau, in state legislatures, and in Congress. For each institution I shall examine how officials recognized, adopted, set a priority for, and maintained interest in, the problem of abuse.

3. The Children's Bureau

In the mid-1950s child abuse slipped quietly onto the agenda of the Children's Bureau (CB), so quietly in fact that it provides a special case for the study of agenda setting. Like the situation in state legislatures and Congress, the CB learned about the problem from issue partisans outside the organization. But unlike legislative efforts, the communication was solely between specialists in child welfare and health without the support and demands of a shocked public. Indeed, the research supported by the CB provided the knowledge base on which public activism and attention were based.

We can go further in describing the special character of the Bureau's initial interest in child abuse. As is often the case in specialized public agencies, problems achieve an organization's agenda without being issues of public policy in the conventionally defined sense. In some instances, government recognizes concerns and chooses to act on them, without the involvement of the mass public. This was certainly true of the CB's recognition and adoption of child abuse.[1]

In this era, the CB was still a professionally respected organization which defined its mission as aiding public and private child health and welfare practitioners and scholars. Over the years it had developed three functions. First, it undertook or sponsored research on pressing problems relating to child health and welfare to determine reasonable, feasible policy responses. Its implicit guiding principle was "action through applied knowledge." But to propose the solutions the Children's Bureau had to discover the problems. Therefore, its second function was to act as a conduit through which professionals exchanged information, particularly the early results of research. Its third function was to make the most current research on child development available to American families. Its most famous pamphlet, *Infant Care*, sold 59 million copies and went through twelve editions. In the first forty years of its existence, *Infant Care* was the second highest selling "book" in the country. Only the Bible was more popular.[2]

In the course of its routine "problem-finding" activities, the Bureau learned of the resurgence of interest in abuse, first from the Children's Division of the American Humane Association (AHA) and several years later from a number of physicians doing medical research on the problem. Abuse was readily acknowledged as the proper concern of child health and welfare professionals and immediately entered the Bureau's communication stream. Achieving this low-level agenda was easy. It took seven years, however, before the issue achieved the CB's research and policy-making agenda. Professionals interested in abuse were fortunate because the Bureau's research budget expanded significantly just as the problem received professional credibility and popular attention. The research funded from the Bureau's regular budget—including the first model child abuse reporting statute—was soon augmented by research supported by a new but permanent appropriation authorized by Congress in 1960. The additional research money and a pressing new research topic gave an increasingly unfashionable organization what may have been its last hour of importance.

"All Matters Pertaining to the Welfare of Children"

The Children's Bureau, established by an act of Congress in 1912, always defined its role to include popularizing information on child development. Unfortunately, the Bureau took its own advice too seriously and popularized the truth out of its own account of its history. In a widely circulated pamphlet, "Your Children's Bureau,"[3] the agency's origins were described without a single reference to the bitter controversy over child labor which both promoted the creation of the Bureau and limited its effectiveness once it was established. Instead, the CB presented a syrupy version of its history, according to which the idea for the agency emerged as Lillian Wald, the founder of New York's Henry Street Settlement, and Florence Kelley, of the National Consumers Union, were enjoying their morning coffee. One day in 1903, the pamphlet says, they received two letters in the mail:

> "Why is it so many children die like flies in the summer time?" one of these letters asked. "Is there something I can do to help matters?" The other was from a mother whose husband had died. She was troubled because, now that she would have to go out to earn support for her children, she would have to place them in an institution.

"There must be thousands of mothers all over the United States in just such situations," observed Miss Wald. "I wish there were some agency that would tell us what can be done about these problems."

Miss Wald and Mrs. Kelley turned to the morning newspaper. The Secretary of Agriculture, the paper reported, was going South that day to find out how much damage the boll weevil was doing to the crops.

That gave Miss Wald an idea.

"If the Government can have a department to take such an interest in what is happening to the Nation's cotton crop, why can't it have a bureau to look after the Nation's crop of children?" she asked.

Miss Wald's idea spread to a friend. He wired it to President Theodore Roosevelt. "Bully!" the President wired back. "Come down and talk to me about it."

Nine years later, on April 9, 1912, the idea had matured into the law that established the Children's Bureau and charged it to investigate and report "upon all matters pertaining to the welfare of children and child life among all classes of our people."[4]

No matter that this sugary description reads remarkably like a passage in R. L. Duffus's equally sugary biography of Lillian Wald.[5] Regardless of possible borrowing, the CB's account of its history was adequate to its task of acquainting the citizenry with the Bureau's activism on behalf of children. Understandably, the Bureau chose to ignore ancient controversies. But these suppressed controversies are important to understanding what kind of issues the Bureau decided to address and its particular brand of response.

In fact, the genesis of the Children's Bureau is found in the battle over child labor which consumed so much of the energies of Progressive Era social reformers. Lillian Wald and Florence Kelley did more than chat over coffee, more too than win the interest of a peripatetic president. President Theodore Roosevelt was an easy convert, believing that the government, like its model—upright men of conscience—had a responsibility to protect women and children.[6] A hostile Congress and a divided Republican party required greater effort.

The battle was aided by the publication of Florence Kelley's famous anti-child-labor essay, *Some Ethical Gains Through Legislation*, which proposed in writing what Kelley had long suggested in her speeches—the creation of a United States Commission for Children.[7] Indeed, child-labor opponents, organized through the

National Child Labor Committee, actually drafted the legislation to establish the Children's Bureau, which was introduced in Congress in 1906.[8] With such controversial proponents, the legislation engendered many adversaries—particularly Southern textile interests and Northern canneries—and did not pass until 1912, three years after President Roosevelt convened the first White House Conference on the Care of Dependent Children. However, it was President William Howard Taft, not Roosevelt, who signed the bill into law.

The act itself, and those who promoted it, left a legacy of problems for the Bureau. The legislation spelled out the Bureau's mandate, and importantly, established *in law* its organizational structure and budget. The mandate was narrow. The act allowed the CB only one task—research, although the scope of acceptable research topics was, in principle, quite wide: "all matters pertaining to the welfare of children and child life among all classes. . . ." A small authorization and some statutory limitations on staff effectively restricted the scope of the research which the Bureau could actually undertake. These limitations made organizational change or growth very difficult, because any change required an amendment to the act proper.

Julia Lathrop, of Hull House fame, moved from Chicago to become the Children's Bureau's first Chief. Though an outsider in Washington, she was known and trusted by child welfare advocates throughout the country. These connections proved to be important in shaping her response to the important dilemmas inherent in creating a new agency.

Early during her tenure Lathrop had to make three important decisions which, like many decisions made when an organization is young and pliable, determined the CB's course for decades to come.[9] First, she chose not to emphasize child labor in the early years of the Bureau's existence. She accepted the advice of Homer Folks, who suggested that such a course was necessary in order to "obviate any possible criticism to the effect that the Federal Children's Bureau is simply an annex of the Child Labor Committee."[10] But Lathrop was committed to the then-radical tenet that every child had a right to a childhood.[11] To achieve this end, she made her second important decision: to proceed gradually and incrementally, undertaking whatever small tasks might aid her vision, working all the while with the help of local experts in voluntary and public child welfare agencies. Just as she sought a partnership with local elites, she sought an equitable division of labor with other federal agencies dealing with children. Her third decision was to define the Bureau's mandate to exclude education and everyday health care and to focus instead on general child welfare and certain public health concerns, particularly as they related to young children. Her first project, a study of birth registration whose purpose was to obtain accurate infant mortality figures, reflected all these decisions.

Each choice which determined policy development for the CB was something of a compromise, but a compromise which Lathrop, an experienced political realist, made with equanimity. The decisions embodied, however, all of the organizational tensions which would plague the CB for years. The first of these tensions was a difficulty in articulating and maintaining a set of enduring concerns. Hostility to the Bureau's anti-child-labor origins lingered, as indeed child labor continued until the Fair Labor Standards Act of 1938 put an end to its worst excesses. (Until 1946, the Children's Bureau supervised that part of the act relating to children.) At the same time, government at all levels became increasingly active in education, health, and welfare. These forces left the Children's Bureau constantly looking for the elusive combination of politically safe yet socially important issues to research. The result was an enduring preference for public health problems with obvious social welfare consequences.

The second tension arose from doing research on the activities of organizations whose help the CB needed in promoting the reforms suggested by the research. Local governments and voluntary groups were often placed in the unenviable position of being asked to cooperate on research which would expose their limitations and mistakes. A good example of this was the CB's efforts to investigate birth registrations. The Bureau recognized that adequate birth registration would promote infant health as well as encourage enforcement of mandatory school attendance and child-labor laws. To encourage complete birth registration, the CB had to articulate the problems with the existing system, annoying if not angering many state and local officials.

The Bureau's methodology, though practical and sound, left a trail of ill-feeling across the country. The CB's own description of the birth registration project shows how unpleasant the research must have been for local officials. "In cooperation with the Bureau, local committees of women canvassed small districts and filled out the standard birth certificate furnished by the Census Bureau. These certificates were then compared with local records and the returns made to the Census Bureau in order to determine the accuracy of birth registrations."[12] The CB offered an alternative to the system it criticized, however. In 1914, it drafted a model state statute on birth registration, consulting in the process with the American Medical Association, the American Public Health Association, and the Bureau of the Census. Promulgating model statutes to rectify health problems became a hallmark of the Bureau's activism on behalf of children.

Clearly the Bureau's research efforts created enemies as well as friends. But the tensions resulting from finding acceptable problems and researching them did not deter the Bureau, which succeeded in most of the projects it undertook. The Bureau, after all, successfully promoted and then administered the Sheppard-Towner Infancy and Maternity Act (1921–29), the federal government's first major grant-in-aid program. Part of the CB's success came from the elliptical way it addressed the economic sources of many social problems.

But the Bureau's early success is attributable to organizational as well as strategic causes. Until 1946, the Bureau reported directly to the Secretary of Labor, so that its voice was not muffled by other, perhaps unsympathetic, speakers.[13] Similarly, in this early period, high-ranking officials in the Children's Bureau were connected to two important, overlapping networks: the Progressive reformers, and for the women, the second generation of female social activists. When the Democrats came to power in 1932, this women's network promoted some of the New Deal's most important social reforms.[14]

The women's network and direct access to the Secretary served to balance the instability generated by a troublesome mandate and an ambivalent clientele. In the 1930s, however, the autonomous voice of the Bureau was threatened by plans to reorganize and downgrade the Bureau, and with this threat began the imperceptible decline of the organization. Steiner reports that the Children's Bureau was not assigned to administer the new Aid to Dependent Children program because of its sloppy preparation of the cost estimates and careless inattention to the need for a caretaker's grant. At the same time President Franklin D. Roosevelt considered, but ultimately decided against, moving the CB out of the Department of Labor and into the newly created Social Security Administration.[15]

The Bureau was not as lucky ten years later. In President Harry S. Truman's massive governmental reorganization in 1946, the CB was moved to the new Federal Security Administration. In a double demotion, the Bureau went from an agency reporting directly to the Secretary of Labor to one of many units reporting to a non-cabinet-level official. Morale in the Bureau was sorely shaken. Three years later, Katherine F. Lenroot, the third Chief of the Children's Bureau, retired. She was replaced by Martha M. Eliot, a physician who joined the CB in 1924 and rose to become Associate Chief.[16]

Eliot belonged to the same generation of social activists as her predecessor Katherine Lenroot. In fact, both were born the same year, 1891. But unlike Lenroot, who was forty-three when she became Chief, Eliot was fifty-eight when she was promoted. The women of the social reform network who enjoyed positions of power and responsibility in the New Deal were, on the average, somewhat older than the men who flocked to Washington for the new experiment in social welfare.[17] But at fifty-eight, Eliot was conspicuously older than her male colleagues in other welfare offices. The commitment to activism, the connection to Progressive Era issues and people, so much an advantage for earlier chiefs, began to seem old-fashioned and out of style. The so-called "problem" continued when Eliot retired in 1957; she was replaced by Katherine B. Oettinger, who was fifty-four when she accepted the position. Oettinger did not belong to the same generation of reformers as Eliot and Lenroot, yet in education, style, and habits she was quite like them. She was committed to social reform as well as (if not more than) to social casework. However, her interests were seen as dated at best.

In 1968, late in the administration of Lyndon B. Johnson, Oettinger (then sixty-five) was promoted to Deputy Assistant Secretary for Population and Family Planning. It was widely believed that her promotion was made to insure that the new Chief of the Children's Bureau would be appointed by a Democratic Administration.[18] But other considerations also affected the timing of the new appointment. The Bureau was under fire within HEW for being old-fashioned and unresponsive to the call to focus on the needs of children on welfare. Career civil servants Mary E. Switzer and Jule M. Sugarman, who supported this redirection of the Bureau's mandate, continued their drive to reorganize the CB into the Nixon administration.

Switzer and Sugarman were successful in their efforts, although the reorganization of the Children's Bureau was part of a larger reorganization in HEW, which sought to impose a more modern management perspective on HEW's enormous and unruly bureaucracy, a bureaucracy staffed by welfare professionals whose support Nixon doubted, with some justification.[20] After some study, HEW Secretary Robert Finch created the Office of Child Development in the Secretary's Office to house the wayward Head Start program (which Congress had removed from the Labor Department), a few struggling child welfare and development experiments, and a chastized Children's Bureau. In this move, the CB lost control of the

Maternal and Child Health program, a grant-in-aid program established by the Social Security Act which was the legislative successor to the Sheppard-Towner Infancy and Maternity Act. This program was moved to the Health Services and Mental Health Administration. Described by one member of the Children's Bureau as "sheer craziness," the reorganization signaled the precipitous decline of a once-proud organization.

Child Abuse and the Children's Bureau

The reorganization came as a cruel and unexpected blow to the Bureau, which had undergone a small renaissance in the preceding ten or fifteen years. The CB's responsibilities had steadily increased since the mid-1950s and it was publicly more visible than at any time since its founding. An increasing interest in physical child abuse contributed to the Bureau's revival.

How did child abuse achieve the CB's agenda? The first part of the story is easy to tell: recognition and adoption were the result of the CB doing what it always did. The Bureau learned of the AHA's interest, and, believing the problem to be serious, lent increasing support to finding a solution.

However, the lasting importance of child abuse to the Bureau, that is to say, the reasons for the issue's increasing priority and sustained maintenance, require more detailed analysis. Child abuse achieved the Children's Bureau's agenda at a time when the agency's research budget was unexpectedly increased, a boon which initially came without legislative directives on how the money had to be spent. An important problem met uncommitted resources and the first generation of child abuse research was born.

Two groups of professionals rediscovered child abuse in the early 1950s, private child-protection specialists and physicians specializing in radiology. Of the two, the private child protection specialists were the first to alert the CB of their interest. But it was the physicians—soon to be dominated by pediatricians—who eventually controlled the issue inside the Bureau and out.

The American Humane Association was established in 1877 to assist in the formation of local humane societies; it added a Children's Division in 1885. Like the SPCCs, the AHA suffered from a loss in public interest and professional prestige as the government's role in child welfare increased. But it was a curious loss in prestige, curious because child welfare professionals in private organizations like SPCCs and the AHA often enjoyed higher status than publicly employed social workers, and private charity was (and is) widely held to be the innovator in child welfare services.[21]

In 1954 the Children's Division of the AHA appointed a new director, Vincent De Francis, an energetic young man fresh from SPCC work in New York. Under his direction, the AHA began a nationwide survey on the existence and extent of services for neglected, abused, and exploited children. In 1956, De Francis published the results in the report *Child Protective Services in the United States*.

De Francis's research employed the traditional SPCC definition of protective services: "bringing help to neglected children—the victims of parents who willfully or unwittingly have endangered their [children's] health, morals, welfare, or emotional development."[22] Physical abuse was not emphasized. Indeed, the prevention and treatment of physical abuse did not take center stage until physicians became interested in this problem.

De Francis was not content with merely publishing the results of the protective services survey. To disseminate the findings he encouraged representatives of national agencies dealing with child protection to reactivate their practice of meeting regularly. At the first of these meetings in 1955, the CB was represented by Annie Lee Sandusky, a black social worker who was the Bureau's specialist on services to children in their own homes.

The CB's participation in this meeting was duly recorded in the Bureau's unpublished *Annual Report*. This brief mention is the first contemporary record of the CB's interest in child protection. With the understatement characteristic of the Children's Bureau, the 1956 *Annual Report* records that there were sharp "differences of opinion amoung [sic] leaders in the protective services field."[23] The controversy focused on the AHA's support of what it called "involuntary" (unwanted) services, or services in the name of the child rather than the adult. At that time, most social workers subscribed to a voluntary, user-initiated approach to services.[24]

De Francis's vision of the proper role of protective services was simultaneously old-fashioned and innovative. On the one hand, it echoed the sentiments of the nineteenth-century child cruelty workers, who not only felt comfortable with deciding the fate of hundreds of poor children but also felt compelled to do so. On the other hand, it presaged two decades of child advocacy efforts. Beginning in the 1960s, lawyers specializing in children's rights increasingly argued for treating the child's needs in abuse and similar cases as separate from the parents'. The Supreme Court's 1967 *In re Gault* opinion, which extended to children Bill of Rights protection, gave force to this view.[25]

Regardless of division of opinion, De Francis's reactivation of regular meetings of child protection advocates was a very shrewd move. Not only were his concerns and opinions directly conveyed to the Children's Bureau, but interested private organizations, including the Child Welfare League, the Family Services Association, the National Council on Crime and Delinquency, United Community Chests and Councils of America, the National Social Work Association, and the American Public Nurse Association, also learned about his work. Activists in the child welfare field quickly recognized that the AHA was energized by new leadership. Thus when the Children's Bureau devoted more attention to the problem of child protective services, many of the affected parties were already cued to the resurgence of interest.

One short entry in an annual report does not indicate that the CB permanently adopted the issue of "child protection," merely that the Bureau recognized that one of its constituents felt the problem was increasingly important. Indeed, the lack of Bureau-generated interest in the subject is evident in the fact that the problem does not appear at all in the 1957 and 1958 *Annual Reports*. In 1959, however, activities related to *child abuse* or *neglect* (the choice of words is the Bureau's) were mentioned twice, the beginning of a trend toward increasing interest in the problem. In 1959, 25.5 lines of the *Annual Report* were devoted to child abuse, and in 1967 202 lines were reserved for the subject, the increase coming in a slightly irregular progression. These entries conclusively show that child abuse had entered the CB's information stream.

In 1960 and 1961 child abuse moved from the information stream to the action agenda, a move which showed its increasing importance within the CB and the Bureau's willingness to maintain an interest in it. The first notice of the Bureau's intention to act more forcefully came in the 1960 *Annual Report:*

> *possible expansion in the scope of the Bureau's work in the area of neglect* may be indicated on the basis of a new development reported in the Regions. Individual members of the medical profession are apparently evincing a quickened interest and concern over the number of children suffering from physical abuse brought to their attention. Several articles were published in medical journals on this subject this past year. The Chief of Pediatrics at the University of Colorado Medical School is making a nation-wide study of the

extent of physical mistreatment of children, including malnutrition or other evidence of serious neglect or abuse. In
Cincinnati, *Ohio*, a meeting was arranged by the Director of
the Children's Hospital and the social agencies to discuss
the problem.[26]

From this point on, the Bureau became firmly committed to research and its particular brand of activism (action through applied
knowledge) on the problem of child abuse. In 1961, the *Annual
Report* discloses that the Bureau compiled an "inventory of public
child welfare agencies providing protective services in each county
and city in the United States."[27]

In 1962, however, the Bureau became deeply engaged in efforts
to come to grips with the "regrettable" problem of physical abuse.[28]
That year, the CB held two meetings, an ad hoc meeting in January
and a planning session in March, to explore "the steps which could
be taken to control child abuse."[29] Though the Bureau first learned
of the problem from child welfare workers, this group was practically invisible at the meetings. Both the ad hoc meeting and the
planning session were chaired by Dr. Arthur Lesser, Director for
Health Services in the CB. Physicians were very much in the fore,
particularly Dr. C. Henry Kempe.

One product of the meetings was the Bureau's model child abuse
reporting law, which was disseminated widely to public and private
child welfare organizations and state legislatures. The Bureau's distribution procedures encouraged the consideration and adoption of
its recommendations. Intuitively, the CB's leaders employed two
tactics which promote the adoption of new ideas. First, the Bureau
was staffed by social workers and public health physicians, and its
audience was similarly comprised. Such professional rapport did
much to make the audience receptive to the CB's new ideas. Second, the Bureau always directed at least part of its attention to child
welfare and health elites by contacting the permanent staff of the
large social service and professional medical organizations. Thus
the "rank and file" in these groups often learned of new ideas or
practices from leaders *inside* their fields. Combined, these two strategies maximized the Bureau's only resource for change, its power
of persuasion. (It is worth noting as well that the AHA employed
similar tactics when presenting the results from its 1956 study of
child protection.)[30]

The two meetings in 1962, along with the model statute (promulgated in 1963), marked an important change in how the Children's Bureau organized its efforts in behalf of abused and neglected

children. Prior to this time, the Bureau discussed child abuse in terms of traditional categories. Child abuse was viewed as only one of several kinds of problems which required protective services. After this time, however, the *Annual Reports* often contain two separate sections on abuse and neglect, one reporting on new developments in child protective services and one reporting on research related to the physical abuse of children.[31]

This bifurcation in reporting reflects more than a stylistic choice by the authors of the *Annual Reports*. Rather, two different versions of the problem had emerged, one grounded in the norms of child welfare practice and the other in the canons of public health medicine. What does not come through in the *Annual Reports*, but is evident from other sources, is that physical abuse in its narrow conception was taking medicine and the media by storm. Physical abuse was portrayed as newly discovered, a disease by virtue of being labeled a "syndrome," and compelling because of its connections with violence. In 1962, it must be remembered, the *Journal of the American Medical Association* published Kempe's article "The Battered-Child Syndrome" and the accompanying editorial.[32]

After writing the model statutes, physicians in the CB did not sustain their interest in, and control over, the problem of physical abuse. At first glance this seems odd because they certainly possessed the power to do so if they wished. But another issue supplanted abuse on their agenda, the study of phenylketonuria (PKU), a hereditary metabolic disease which causes mental retardation if left untreated. John F. Kennedy, whose sister Rosemary was retarded, brought an interest in retardation to his presidency. This concern was translated into research money through the Maternal and Child Welfare Amendments of 1963. PKU, which also strikes children, had the same public appeal as physical abuse, but the biochemical research required to find its remedy was much more within the tradition of medical science than any research on abuse could ever be. Thus the Health Services Division of the CB shifted its interest to PKU, to solve an important problem, but also, as one observer noted, "to enhance research on crippled children which suffered from low status."

While physicians within the Health Services Division were occupied with another issue, the Welfare Division initiated a series of child abuse research projects which focused on social services questions. In 1962, Dr. Charles Gershenson, a mathematical psychologist who had been the research director at the Jewish Children's Bureau of Chicago, came to the U.S. Children's Bureau to set up a Child Welfare Research Bureau. Under his aegis, the CB awarded research grants for a wide variety of projects in the areas of child abuse and family law. Some were unfruitful, but others—notably David Gil's research which was reported in *Violence Against Children*—provided the benchmark data on attitudes about and strategies to combat physical abuse.[33] The cost of these studies is enormously difficult to ascertain because most of the documents were destroyed when the Bureau was reorganized in 1969. Over a five- or six-year period, however, Gershonson, who managed the projects, estimates that the CB's research expenditures on child abuse and related family law projects alone amounted to well over a million dollars.

The large investment in research projects shows the high priority of child abuse within the CB and guaranteed the issue's maintenance on the agenda. Each research project produced many reports, and each report increased the Bureau's interest in the subject, because each contained exciting, new information available nowhere else. In the years between 1955 and 1967, child abuse became a staple concern of the Children's Bureau, and the CB became even better known within professional child welfare circles for sponsoring research on important and current problems.

Interpreting the Bureau's Interest in Child Abuse

To understand the Children's Bureau's increased interest in child protective services and physical child abuse, we must remember that these were not considered new issues by the Bureau in the same way the problems—especially abuse—were considered to be newly discovered by state legislatures and Congress. These issues came well within the Bureau's mandate. Their recognition and adoption represented a routine shift in emphasis in an organization whose job was to discern the nation's major child health and welfare problems. As the Bureau carried out its mandate, it became aware of the AHA's revived interest in child protection, and later the concern of the Denver physicians with physical child abuse. Proud of keeping up-to-date, the Bureau regularly reported these new developments through publications and participation in meetings.

But it was more than a self-defined role as an "issue-sensing" organization which allowed the CB so easily to recognize, adopt, and maintain a vigorous interest in these issues. The Bureau was able to give so much attention to child protection, physical abuse, and ultimately child neglect because the problems emerged on the agenda exactly, and fortuitously, at the same time that the Bureau was infused with new resources for research. At first these resources were completely unfettered. Over time, however, both the research agenda of the Bureau and its management capacities became taxed with new demands, including statutorily mandated research on maternal and child health problems, and administrative responsibility for a much enlarged set of Maternal and Child Welfare grant-in-aid programs. Ultimately these demands—and an altered political climate within the Department of Health, Education, and Welfare—contributed to the Bureau's decline.

A little-known provision of the 1960 Amendments to the Social Security Act provided the research resources which were channeled into studying child abuse. Without this money the CB would not have been able to maintain such a strong commitment to the problem. And since it was the research sponsored by the Bureau which sustained professional commitment, and professional commitment which in turn sustained public interest, it is critical to investigate the infusion of research funds.

When the Social Security Act first passed in 1935, the Children's Bureau's responsibilities grew. In addition to its mandate to investigate problems of child health and welfare, it became responsible for administering Title V of the act: Grants to the States for Maternal and Child Welfare. At that time three programs were included under this title: maternal and child health services, crippled children's services, and child welfare services.[34] Originally the formula for dispersing funds under Title V favored rural areas where private children's services were less developed. In 1958, the rural bias was eliminated and a more equitable variable grant formula instituted. But more importantly, the 1958 amendments established a one-year Advisory Council on Child Welfare Services to suggest new directions for child welfare services policy. Among other things, the Council recommended an increase in funding and personnel for "grants to research organizations, institutions of higher learning, and public and voluntary social agencies for demonstration and research projects in child welfare."[35]

Such favorable recommendations were not at all surprising. The members of the Council were all child welfare specialists handpicked by the Children's Bureau for their well-known support of the Bureau's activities. (One of them, Fred DelliQuadri, later became Chief of the Bureau). What is somewhat more startling is that the research recommendation was enacted in the 1960 Social Security Amendments, giving the Bureau one million dollars in additional research funds, but no specific mandate except that it be spent on "projects . . . which show promise of substantial contribution to the advancement of child welfare."[36]

This windfall was possible because, compared to the figures usually discussed in Social Security hearings, one million dollars for child welfare research was trivial. In 1960 members of the Senate Finance Committee and the House Ways and Means Committee were consumed with the debates over national health insurance. Small concessions to minor programs barely touched them. But if unimportant to Congress, the money was crucial to the Children's Bureau, which encouraged Martha Eliot, then recently retired as Chief, to testify in favor of the Maternal and Child Welfare Amendment which contained this provision. By accepting this amendment, Congress unknowingly bankrolled a whole new era for the Children's Bureau.

The importance of these research funds to the Children's Bureau as an organization, and its interest in child abuse as a problem, cannot be overestimated. Quite simply, the 1960 Maternal and Child Welfare Amendment gave the CB a vastly increased research capacity, and, importantly, radically changed its style of research. For example, in fiscal year 1962, the first year that the "new" research money was available, child welfare research expenditures under the 1960 amendments were $219,000. This money provided two-thirds again the total amount spent for research that year, the Bureau having spent $349,000 for research out of its regular appropriation. Moreover, the amount of research money available under the 1960 amendments increased by leaps and bounds. In 1966, the last year the budget distinguishes between CB expenditures for research out of its own budget and expenditures funded from the child welfare research (1960) amendments, the Bureau spent $537,000 on research from its budget proper compared with $7,999,000 authorized by the 1960 amendments.[37] Indeed, by this time the CB was also administering research funds targeted to problems of maternal and child health and crippled children. The Bureau's total research expenditures from sources outside its own budget approached $12,000,000 in 1966.[38]

These research efforts funded through Title V became the tail that wagged the dog. A fifty-year tradition of in-house research ended. Prior to 1962 most of the CB's research was conducted by its staff. The money available through the 1960 amendment ended this practice. In 1962 the Bureau hired Charles Gershenson to coordinate the new child welfare research efforts. Though an able scholar himself, Gershenson's job was to coordinate the research efforts of others. The Children's Bureau more or less stopped engaging in original research. Consequently, the studies were technically more sophisticated than work that had been or could be conducted in-house. Another perhaps more important consequence was that the Bureau had delegated to outsiders one of its most important functions, indeed, the purpose for which it had been created: to *investigate* and report on all matters pertaining to the welfare of children.

An agency of researchers became an agency of grant managers, and the number and variety of grants overseen by the Bureau expanded rapidly; far more rapidly than the slowly increasing staff could absorb. Practically every year during the 1960s, the Children's Bureau's mandate grew. In 1960, the Social Security amendments added the child welfare research responsibility. After that there was no stopping Congress and the Bureau. Service grants or research programs on maternal and child health, crippled children, mental retardation, juvenile delinquency, day care, maternity and infant care, training child welfare professionals, and preschool and school-age children's health programs crowded the CB's agenda. The CB actively sought some of the programs and merely accepted others in a spiral of exhilaration and frenzy. The administrative capacity of the organization was sorely taxed, however. Between 1960 and 1967, when the Bureau was melded into Social and Rehabilitative Services in an effort to make it more responsive to "special populations," the staff had increased by 65.7% from 254 to 421, whereas the budgets of the Children's Bureau and Maternal and Child Health programs combined increased a hundredfold from $2.3 million to $239.3 million.[39]

With this legislative history in mind, it is easy to see why child abuse became such an important component of the Bureau's research agenda. Child abuse fit precisely into the mold of issues favored by the Bureau—public health issues with a strong social welfare component. In fact, the CB's immediate response to physical child abuse was to promulgate a model state reporting statute, precisely the same tactic the Bureau used in responding to its first problem—adequate birth registration. But unlike birth registration, most of the Bureau's research was conducted *after* the model act was proposed. Moreover, the extraordinary amount of research sponsored by the CB was made possible because child abuse was on the frontier of child welfare issues at a time when the CB had an enormously expanded and unencumbered research budget. By establishing a network of researchers whose careers were enhanced by child abuse research—including David Gil, Andrew Billingsley, Jeanne Giovannoni, Howard Freeman, and Vincent De Francis— the Bureau kept child abuse on its agenda and the public's agenda, in an ever-widening circle. But the administrative problems of the Bureau's enlarged mandate were soon to swamp the organization.

The Rise of Child Abuse and Decline of the Children's Bureau

Quite simply, the Bureau had too much to do, even though from most contemporary accounts high officials in HEW were not displeased with the quality of the CB's work but rather with its legislative mandate to study a specific population—children—rather than a problem, and importantly, its stiff-necked style.

The tension between population-oriented social programs and problem-oriented ones was never far from the surface in HEW. The earliest public response to welfare problems had been organized largely by populations of beneficiaries, with veterans being the best example. Many kinds of assistance—payments, services, referrals and the like—frequently were administered by one agency. The Children's Bureau, though much more limited in mandate, was organized in this manner. In the late 1960s, the Bureau, and the philosophy which underpinned it, became increasingly unpopular. Modern management of welfare bureaucracies dictated a change toward functional rather population-centered organization.[40] To people like Wilbur Cohen, then Assistant Secretary for Legislation, there seemed to be every reason to blend the Children's Bureau's functions into other administrative units.

The movement toward administration by function had been underway in HEW since early in the decade. In 1963, Secretary Anthony Celebrezze removed the administration of the welfare (ADC) program from the Social Security Administration. He established a new Welfare Administration, housing the Bureau of Family Services (ADC programs), the Office of Aging, the Office of Juvenile Delinquency, and the Children's Bureau. At the same time, the Office of Vocational Rehabilitation was upgraded to the Vocational Rehabilitation Administration. These moves themselves did not signal an immediate change in the Bureau's fortunes.

In 1967, however, HEW began a second series of administrative reorganizations from which the CB never recovered. On August 15, 1967, Secretary John W. Gardner, an even stronger supporter of administration by function, announced the creation of the Social and Rehabilitative Service out of the Welfare Administration, the Vocational Rehabilitation Administration, and the Administration on Aging. It was organized into five major divisions: the Assistance Payment Administration, the Medical Services Administration, the Administration on Aging, the Rehabilitative Services Administration, and the Children's Bureau. Mary E. Switzer, the successful, intensely political director of the Vocational Rehabilitation Administration, was placed at the helm. Unlike earlier reorganizations, this effort was aimed directly at undercutting the Bureau, which was felt to be too set in its prissy social worker ways. Katherine Oettinger (age 65) was promoted to Deputy Assistant Secretary for Population and Family Planning, and the much sought after "younger person," Fred DelliQuadri (age 53!), was appointed, but not without a long search and a break with the tradition which had designated this position as a woman's job.[41] This period of administrative no-confidence coincided with the addition of the largest task ever assigned to the Bureau. The 1967 Social Security Amendments, passed on January 2, 1968, and effective July 1, 1968, moved the Child Welfare Services program authorized under Grants to States for Maternal and Child Welfare (Title V) to Title IV, the Public Assistance (AFDC) program, which also offered social services, but only to AFDC recipients. Congress gave this expanded service program to the Children's Bureau to run.

In point of fact, the CB never actually "ran" the program, although it was titularly in the CB's control. No meaningful direction was offered because six months after the responsibility began the new administration of President Richard M. Nixon, in the person of HEW Secretary Robert Finch, reorganized the Children's Bureau again. The Bureau was too shaken to do anything more than push the appropriate papers around. When this reorganization was complete, a stripped-down Children's Bureau, with about twenty employees in Washington, was housed in the Office of Child Development, with Head Start and a few unimportant child welfare and development experiments.

This Children's Bureau was stripped of almost every task for which it had been established. Not only did the Bureau lose responsibility for the newly combined child welfare services, it also lost its traditional Maternal and Child Welfare Programs, which went to the Health Services and Mental Health Administration in a move motivated by functional efficiency. The great expansion of child welfare research had been financed under the Maternal and Child Welfare programs, so the Bureau's research budget was also gutted. The CB had changed its own research activities from in-house research to grants management and would never again reestablish its scholarly or policy-making reputation. The surest sign of its tarnished prestige was evident from the fact that an agency which had five chiefs in fifty-four years has not been able to keep a chief appointed from the outside for more than two years since the 1968 reorganization.

Through its own budget, the CB retained a tiny research presence in the years after the 1968 reorganization, but the damage to morale killed any initiative which might have survived the budget cuts. Virtually no child abuse research was being funded by the CB per se, although the problem had been deemed important by so many disciplines—and the public at large—that funding from other sources, including the Titles IV and V programs the Children's Bureau used to administer, was available.

Indeed, the Children's Bureau might have ceased to exist in anything other than name if Congress had not passed the Child Abuse Prevention and Treatment Act in 1974. The act established a National Center for Child Abuse and Neglect (NCCAN), and NCCAN was housed in the Children's Bureau. But even more than before, this tail seemed to wag the dog. In this instance the Bureau had only limited imput into the research sponsored by NCCAN. With the irony of politics, the federal child abuse legislation, the direct descendant of the CB's research efforts, kept the Children's Bureau alive. The federal legislation depended in part, however, on public interest in the problem. How the media fostered that interest is the subject of the next chapter.

4. The Agenda-Setting Function of the Media

What part did the media play in transforming the once-minor charity concern called "cruelty to children" into an important social welfare issue? We would expect the media's role to be very important, because the media exist at the boundary between the private and the public. Their task is to discover, unveil, and create what is "public." To do so they often wrench "private deviance" from the confines of the home. In the case of child abuse the media also helped to establish a new area of public policy.

This chapter examines how the media both *created* and *responded to* the urgency over child abuse. This cycle was inevitable because child abuse achieved many agendas—in the federal bureaucracy, state legislatures, and Congress—during a period of almost twenty years. Not surprisingly, the media's role varied, sometimes prodding governmental action, at other times passively reporting governmental interest.

Our first task is to discuss the media's "issue-attention cycle," modifying Anthony Downs's pioneering work on the subject.[1] Downs suggests a shortish issue-attention cycle for the mass media, although he never actually specifies a particular length of time for the transition from popularity to eclipse. In the nineteenth century the media's attention to cruelty to children followed Downs's short-attention-span model. But in the last twenty years professional and popular interest in abuse has increased steadily, in a manner unanticipated by Downs's formulation. The link between the professional and mass media—where the professional media pump new information to the mass media—helps to explain the mass media's enduring interest.

Our second task is to analyze the history of professional coverage of child abuse, its emergence in popular magazines, and the role of newspapers in sustaining coverage and thus maintaining general interest. Here we shall find that magazines and newspapers initially showed a preference for reporting cases of bizarre brutalization, giving journalists the opportunity to act as the child's advocate against the crime of parenting gone crazy. More recently, both sources, but particularly newspapers, have added many articles reporting research findings. These human interest (as opposed to crime) stories account for much of the newspapers' sustained interest in the problem.

The "Issue-Attention Cycle"

In order to gain a full understanding of the media's role, we must examine how political issues are usually covered by the media, particularly how and when coverage of an issue is sustained. Anthony Downs has presented the most compelling description of the "issue-attention cycle" to date.[2] Downs predicts that problems begin to fade from the media's and the public's attention when their solutions imply the necessity of economic redistribution, or when media coverage begins to bore an ever-restless public. As mentioned above, nineteenth-century coverage of the problem conforms to Downs's formulation, but, perhaps surprisingly, twentieth-century coverage does not. Rather than fading from prominence, child abuse has received constant, even growing, attention from the media. Careful investigation into *how* and *why* the media covered child abuse at various times leads us to revise Downs's issue-attention cycle. As we shall see, it appears that issues can have a much longer attention cycle than previously supposed, a finding which has important consequences, one of which is that political agendas become increasingly crowded, a fact significant for the real and perceived efficiency of government.

Just as there are many more issues, concerns, and conflicts than government can address, there are many more potential stories than the media can report. The problem of deciding "what's news" is severe. Tom Wilkinson, Metro Editor for the *Washington Post*, has written that "the *Washington Post*, like other large media outlets receives approximately one million words every day . . . [and] has the capacity to publish about 100,000 words—or 10 percent of the information received. Competition for space is fierce."[3]

Scholarly research on how the media decide which problems are important has focused primarily on the congruence between issues deemed important by the media and those judged salient by individuals, especially at election time.[4] The electoral emphasis of this research is unfortunate because specific social issues often cannot be associated with a particular party, making it unlikely they would be absorbed in campaign coverage.[5] Downs's interest in the life cycle of issues stands as an important exception to the body of research focusing on the agenda-setting function of the media in elections. He presents a five-step outline detailing what he calls the issue-attention cycle. First, Downs suggests, there is the pre-problem stage, where the objective conditions of the problem are often more severe and pervasive than in the second stage, called "alarmed discovery and euphoric enthusiasm." With deadly accuracy, Downs notes that Americans have a touching blend of horrified concern and wide-eyed, cotton-candy confidence which leads them to assert "that every problem can be solved . . . *without any fundamental reordering of society itself.*"[6] Government begins to try to solve the problem at this point. Soon, however, the initial enthusiasm for solving the problem gives way to the third stage, a more sober realization that significant progress will be costly not only in terms of money but also in terms of social stability. When the need for redistribution or social reordering seems to be part of the solution to a particular problem, Downs suggests that the cycle enters its fourth stage, where both the media and their audiences begin to loose interest. In step five an issue enters the "post-problem stage." Whatever response has been initiated by government becomes institutionalized. Once innovative and exciting programs become part of the business-as-usual processes of government. The issue retains routine coverage, but the public, hungry for novel news, implicitly demands a new set of issues.

Intuitively, Downs's description of the issue-attention cycle seems to be accurate. Certainly the cognoscenti of the media, the regular readers, listeners, and viewers, sense the pattern of the media's (and government's) attention to particular issues. Downs's formulation has not been put to the test, however. Indeed, it is difficult to do so because his objective was to sketch the overall pattern of the issue-attention cycle, not to specify its processes. By attempting to understand child abuse coverage in terms of Downs's formulation, we learn a great deal about what sustains media interest and coverage.

The Mary Ellen Case

Downs's issue-attention cycle aptly describes media, public, and governmental interest in child maltreatment at the point when the problem was "discovered" in 1874, and when the now-familiar Mary Ellen case tugged at the hearts of fashionable New York. It is fair to say that without media coverage of the Mary Ellen case, child protection might never have become institutionalized as a social problem distinct from the Scientific Charity movement's more general interest in reducing sloth, pauperism, and dependence on the public purse. Without a doubt the living and working conditions of many children during the Gilded Era conform to Downs's pre-problem stage. The misery of poverty and a tradition of legal and religious precepts supporting a father's right to raise a child as he saw fit probably made violence toward children fairly prevalent. The ideal of a protected childhood, which encouraged the recognition of child abuse as a social problem, was just beginning to develop.

It was the Mary Ellen case, however, which ushered in the second stage of "alarmed discovery and euphoric enthusiasm."[7] In the spring of 1874 the *New York Times*[8] and the other New York papers reported that Mary Ellen Wilson had been chained to her bed and whipped daily with a rawhide cord by her stepmother. The *Times* was not yet governed by the motto "All the News Fit to Print," which was adopted in 1897.[9] Nonetheless, the *Times* only rarely carried stories about cases of even such blatant abuse as that suffered by Mary Ellen, and even when the *Times* did cover such stories, it was in a tone much more moderate than that used by papers with larger circulations such as the *New York Herald* and the *World*. In fact, the *Times* covered only one other instance of a child similarly abused in the two years prior to Mary Ellen's case.

Even Mary Ellen's story might never have become part of the public record had not Henry Bergh been informed of the abuse by "a lady who had been on an errand of mercy to a dying woman in the house adjoining [Mary Ellen's]."[10] The ensuing trial of Mary Ellen's stepmother, who received a one-year penitentiary term, and the decision about what to do with Mary Ellen, who was eventually sent to the Sheltering Arms children's home, remained in the news through June of that year. As 1874 drew to a close, Mary Ellen's plight reemerged in the *Times*, this time as the reason for the formation of the New York Society for the Prevention of Cruelty to Children (New York SPCC), the nation's first charitable organization dedicated to identifying ill-treated children.

Of course, the Mary Ellen case was not the first instance of cruelty to children to receive newspaper coverage. The bizarre brutalization of children and public horror over it always received a modicum of attention in the press. The significance of the Mary Ellen case rests with its label—cruelty to children—which like the later labels unified seemingly unrelated cases, and in the fact that it precipitated the formation of an organization whose purpose was to keep this issue alive.

The label "cruelty to children" and the Mary Ellen case did not, however, ensure sustained media attention. Two measures of the issue's rapid decline from prominence can be garnered from the *New York Times Index*. In the 1874 volume of the *Index* the entry "Children, Cruelty to" appears for the first time. However, this subject entry disappears from the *Index* beginning in July, 1877, and does not reappear until 1885, after which time it occurs only infrequently until World War I. During the first three years of recognition, the *Times* published fifty-two news articles it specifically categorized as dealing with "cruelty to children." But the deletion of the cruelty to children subject heading did not signal the end of coverage of the topic. By searching all the subject entries about children, articles on child abuse cases and the activities of prevention societies can be found. Most frequently, instances of abuse and neglect are classified under the ignominious heading "Children, miscellaneous facts about." In the judgment of librarians of that period, cruelty to children ceased to be a problem important enough to warrant special reference.

A century later, it is difficult to determine whether the issue's short tenure in the spotlight was indeed caused by the reason Downs suggests, i.e., that a meaningful response to the problem includes a major revamping of society. Certainly, a concerted response to child abuse must include an examination and reordering of economic and social arrangements—a protected childhood is not possible without it. But it was the Progressives and not the Scientific Charity advocates who posed the important structural questions. Prevention societies like those in New York City managed to blind themselves to one of the important functions of their work: imposing middle-class familial values on the poor without changing their economic circumstances. (The prevention societies did of course help to remove a large number of women and children from truly abusive or neglectful circumstances. Whether the women who returned to their husbands or the children who were placed in dreary, regimented orphanages thought their lot was improved is a question which cannot easily be answered.)

A problem can fade from center stage even if it does not involve questions of economic redistribution. From the beginning of the protective society movement, the "child savers" were divided over whether physical punishment of a child constituted cruelty. The conflict surfaced at the very first meeting of the New York Society for the Prevention of Cruelty to Children, when Henry Bergh "took exception to Mr. [Elbridge] Gerry calling a father who ill treated his child a 'brute.' . . . While anxious to protect children from undue severity, [Bergh] said he was in favor of a good wholesome flogging, which he often found most efficacious."[11]

This tension over the appropriateness of the physical punishment of children must have affected the "child savers" personally as well as organizationally. Indeed, the prevention societies' insistence on limiting their task to identifying and labeling maltreatment among the working class and the poor may indicate the strength of their own ambivalence over physical punishment. In addition, the SPCCs' choice to limit their role to casefinding also created a permanent organizational instability. Any charity like the SPCCs, whose sole job was to find cases, always risked being undermined by the groups who provided more long-term services. Charities providing services would eventually want to control their own casefinding because in so doing they could better promote their own success. SPCC workers rendered both the psychological tension and organizational imbalance more bearable by projecting these problems onto abusers— poor and working-class people who were sufficiently different and socially inferior to provide some psychic relief to the middle-class child savers who uneasily took it upon themselves to point their fingers at others.[12]

Contemporary Media Coverage

It is no surprise, then, that after the novelty of the Mary Ellen case wore off, newspapers and professional journals gave the problem only sporadic coverage. Indeed, almost ninety years elapsed before the issue again took center stage in the media, in the form of the now-famous article "The Battered-Child Syndrome" by Dr. C. Henry Kempe and his associates, published in the July 7, 1962 issue of the *Journal of the American Medical Association*.[13] With the publication of this article, a tiny trickle of information grew into a swollen river, flooding mass-circulation newspapers and magazines and professional journals alike. In the decade prior to the article's appearance doctors, lawyers, social workers, educators and other researchers and practitioners combined published only nine articles specifically focusing on cruelty to children. In the decade after its publication, the professions produced 260 articles. Similarly, mass-circulation magazines carried twenty-eight articles in the decade after Kempe's article, compared to only three in the decade before, two of which recounted instances of bizarre brutalization.[14]

Even televison displayed an interest in the problem. Although it is harder to document this medium fully, it seems that child abuse was virtually absent from early televison scripts, whereas after "The Battered-Child Syndrome" appeared, soap operas and prime-time series alike created dramas based on the problem. The plight of

Mary Ellen's fictional brothers and sisters was first beamed into millions of households in episodes of *Dr. Kildare, Ben Casey, M.D.,* and *Dragnet.*[15]

These figures on the emergence of child abuse in the media suggest that Downs's formulation of the issue-attention cycle needs to be amended. Contrary to Downs's hypothesis, media attention to child abuse grew steadily rather than declined, and the public has sustained a loyal interest in what might on the surface be thought of as a small, even unimportant, issue. Admittedly, Downs does not speculate on how long the issue-attention cycle takes to run its course. Nonetheless, findings so strikingly at variance with the tenor of Downs's formulation deserve closer attention.

Four factors contribute to the continuing coverage of child abuse and suggest that media attention to a host of issues can be more long-lived than previously assumed. These factors include topic differentiation, isssue aggregation, the link between the professional and the mass media, and the growing appeal of human interest stories (especially ones with a medical deviance twist).

First and foremost, coverage of abuse increased because stories about *specific types* of abuse were added to the earlier, more general reports. In other words, coverage increased because the general problem of abuse was differentiated into more narrowly defined topics such as the relationship between illegitimacy and abuse, or abuse within military families.[16] Second, child abuse coverage increased because the issue was also linked with larger, more overarching concerns, such as intrafamilial violence, which now includes abuse of a spouse, parent, or even grandparent.[17] The scope of the problem is thus simultaneously decreasing and increasing.

Topic differentiation and issue aggregation are themselves explained by a third factor which encourages sustained media attention to child abuse. To a large extent the mass media carefully and consistently monitor professional and scientific journals in search of new stories. This symbiotic relationship is perhaps the most neglected factor contributing to ongoing media coverage of issues. Despite the lack of attention paid to it, the relationship between the mass media and professional outlets is well institutionalized, and serves both parties admirably, providing fresh stories for journalists and (for the most part) welcome publicity for scholars. Moreover, this relationship provides a regular source of "soft (i.e., interesting) news" about child abuse. Indeed, the fourth factor contributing to the durability of child abuse coverage is the fact that "soft news"—human interest stories—has been added to "hard news" stories, which have traditionally focused on child abuse cases as crime news. This last factor should not be confused with the first two. Soft news stories extend the range of story *types*, whereas differentiation and aggregation extend the range of story *topics*.

By investigating each of these factors we can show how media coverage both created the demand for, and was a product of, governmental action. The first three factors—differentiation, aggregation, and the relationship between the professional and mass media—can be considered together. These three factors are linked through the recognition that child abuse was initially a research issue, and that research on a problem has a life cycle of its own. This life cycle can greatly affect the prominence of an issue in the media.

As chapter 3 has shown, physical abuse was a research problem long before it was a public policy issue in the conventional sense. During the decade between 1946 and 1957 radiologists reluctantly pieced together evidence revealing that a fair number of children had bruises and broken bones, the cause of which could only be parental violence. This research, however, never crossed the bridge from scientific publications to the mass media. Indeed, not until 1960 did the Children's Bureau even mention these medical studies in its *Annual Report*.[18]

Much has been made of the fact that the radiological research failed to create a stir outside roentgenological circles. The cause is often attributed to the low status of radiology within medicine, and, in fact, only one of the early articles was published in the prestigious AMA *Journal*. But importantly, this article—by P. V. Woolley and W. A. Evans, Jr.—stopped short of crediting injuries to willful parental violence.[19] Instead the authors suggested that the injuries were due to "indifference, immaturity and irresponsibility of parents."[20] Thus it was more than the low status of radiologists which kept the social origins of physical abuse from being determined; it was also a pronounced distaste for acknowledging parental behavior so at odds with the ideal.

In 1962 the situation changed, however. Dr. C. Henry Kempe and his colleagues published "The Battered-Child Syndrome" in the AMA *Journal*. The article and its companion editorial caused a storm in medical circles and in the mass media as well. Indeed, the article and editorial are routinely used to date the rediscovery of abuse. In this instance, medical research and opinion did cross the bridge to the mass media, primarily through the vehicle of the AMA press release "Parental Abuse Looms in Childhood Deaths."[22] The message of the article and editorial was clear: Kempe and his co-workers had "discovered" an alarming and deadly "disease" which menaced the nation's children. The article was measured in tone and

eminently professional, although its findings were later sensation-
alized through less careful retelling. But the editorial presented
problems from the beginning.

The most important characteristic of the article is that it provided
a powerful, unifying label in the phrase "the battered-child syndrome." Kempe purposefully chose the term to emphasize the medical, and downplay the criminal, aspects of the problem. The year
before, as a hardworking member of the American Pediatric Association's convention program committee, he had the opportunity to
organize a panel on any topic he chose. Naturally he chose the topic
of his current research, the physical abuse of children. Colleagues
warned him, however, that a panel using that title might scare away
just the audience he sought to inform. Kempe agreed and changed
the title to "The Battered-Child Syndrome." As it turned out, his
choice of label was inspired. Like others who promoted the issue,
Kempe saw the need to diffuse anxiety and promote consensus
through the choice of a nonthreatening label. For the same kinds
of reasons, legislators frequently employed the term "child abuse,"
which conjured up severe maltreatment yet avoided any taint of
association with "discipline."

The editorial was equally powerful but more problematic. Based
on what would now be considered very dubious epidemiological
evidence, the editors of the AMA *Journal* proclaimed: "It is likely
that [the battered-child syndrome] will be found to be a more frequent cause of death than such well recognized and thoroughly
studied diseases as leukemia, cystic fibrosis and muscular dystrophy
and may well rank with automobile accidents."[23] Then as now, the
difficulties in determining accurate figures about child abuse, even
mortality figures, were enormous. The death rate may have been
as high as the editors presumed, perhaps even higher, but they
could not have known that with certainty using existing data. However, supported by data or not, the editors annointed the problem
with the most durable of unctions: they established the significance
of the problem by asserting its frequency.

The AMA's news release repeated Kempe's findings and the *Journal*'s opinion to a wider audience. Like many professional associations, the AMA routinely issues press releases about important
findings reported in its journal. This practice constitutes the first
link in a chain which keeps mass media personnel abreast of medical, scientific, and technical developments. At the other end of the
chain are the beat reporters who cultivate the sources behind the
news releases. The chain, little studied in the policy-making lit-

erature but well institutionalized, transmitted Kempe's findings to journalists responsible for medical news.

Within a week of the news release, *Time* magazine summarized the article as the second feature in its "Medicine" section. (The lead medical article, garnered from the *Medical Letter*, and the AMA *Journal*, touted the fact that oral contraceptives "have proved to be 'virtually 100% effective.' ") *Newsweek*, however, beat *Time* to the punch. In the April 16, 1962 edition of *Newsweek*, the findings of "The Battered-Child Syndrome" were reported. This article coincided with the fiftieth anniversary of the Children's Bureau. Although the exact origins of this article are no longer known, its genesis appears to have been a celebratory news release by the Children's Bureau. Together, *Time* and *Newsweek* informed millions of readers that a new "disease" imperiled the nation's children.[24]

If these two magazines informed a somewhat selective and small audience, the *Saturday Evening Post* and *Life* had more popular appeal. The *Post* published an article entitled "Parents Who Beat Children: A Tragic Increase in Cases of Child Abuse Is Prompting a Hunt for Ways to Select Sick Adults Who Commit Such Crimes" on October 6, 1962.[25]

Like the news magazine articles, the author of the *Post*'s article interviewed the medical experts: Kempe, and other physicians such as Dr. Vincent Fontana, Chief of Pediatrics at New York's St. Vincent's Hospital, Dr. Frederic N. Silverman, chief radiologist at Cincinnati Children's Hospital (and one of the coauthors of "The Battered-Child Syndrome") and Dr. John L. Gwenn, radiologist at Los Angeles Children's Hospital. The Chief of the Children's Bureau, Mrs. Katherine Oettinger, and her deputy, Dr. Katherine Bain, were also interviewed. But in the *Post* article, these interviews were juxtaposed with a recitation of the gory details of child abuse.

Charles Flato wrote the *Post* article, in which he leaned heavily on the *Newsweek* piece written but not signed by current "Medicine" editor Matthew Clark. No highbrow restraint fettered Flato in the *Post* article. On the first page of this article in a respected family magazine, Flato unleashed his journalistic talents to describe abuse:

> In the United States generally, at least two children a day are savagely assaulted by their own parents. The most common form of parental abuse is beating. The second is burning—with matches, cigarettes or electric irons, or by holding the child's hands, arms or feet over an open flame. Many are

deliberately scalded with whatever happens to be bubbling on the stove.

Others are strangled, thrown, dropped, shot, stabbed, shaken, drowned, suffocated, sexually violated, held under running water, tied upright for long periods of time, stepped on, bitten, given electric shocks, forced to swallow pepper or buried alive. The reports of the injuries read like a case book of a concentration-camp doctor: bruises, contusions, welts, skull fractures, broken bones, brain injuries, burns, concussions, cuts, gashes, gunshot and knife wounds, ruptured vital organs, bites, dislocated necks, asphyxiations, eyes gouged out.[26]

The list of types of abuse, its length, detail, and thesaurus-like completeness, could only inflame readers—so too, the reference to a concentration camp, a reference with uncanny and probably unknown significance. Charles Flato was probably unaware that C. Henry Kempe had fled Nazi Germany. The article goes beyond the inflammatory, however. Flato also describes the difficulty encountered in the treatment of child abuse cases, which was then believed to stem from the absence of laws requiring the reporting of child abuse. The article concludes with an upbeat note that the Children's Bureau "has drafted a model [reporting] law for submission to state legislatures" to remedy the problem.[27]

In a double-barreled shot, photojournals and news magazines introduced child abuse to the American public. The articles can be considered the point at which an invisible problem became a public concern, and soon a major public policy issue. The popular agenda was set and the problem was defined as one of medical deviance—the broader concerns went unmentioned.

If the simplicity of the medical deviance construction of abuse was unrealistic, it was nonetheless useful in capturing the public's attention. For the next twenty years, popular magazines began what seemed to be a campaign to publicize the problem. The *Readers' Guide to Periodical Literature* cites 124 articles published from 1960 through 1980. As figure 4.1 shows, the articles cluster around significant research breakthroughs and political events. But the tempo of coverage was constant. Abuse has remained a staple in popular magazines as different as *Woman's Day* and *Scientific American*.

The durability of coverage was in part caused by new "events" (research or action) which continually revitalized interest. Thus Downs underestimated the extent to which his formulation assumed that individual or closely clustered events trigger the issue-

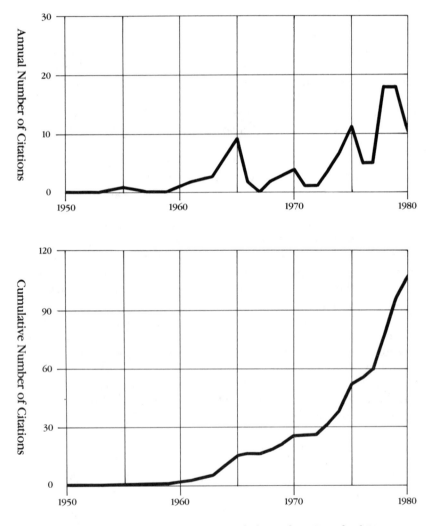

Figure 4.1. Source: *Reader's Guide to Periodical Literature.*

attention cycle. Though every professional article did not get the recognition of "The Battered-Child Syndrome," over *1,700* articles on child abuse or related subjects have been published in professional journals over the last thirty years. Together they kept a steady stream of information flowing to beat reporters and issue partisans. In many ways, 1,700 professional articles represented 1,700 events to be investigated, if not actually reported.

The volume of professional research on abuse and related topics is staggering, and grew exponentially for precisely the reasons (issue differentiation and aggregation) mentioned before. Figure 4.2 portrays this explosion of professional interest. *Index Medicus* lists *1,235* articles in English from 1950 to 1980, only one of which was published prior to 1962. Similarly, the *Education Index* reports 238 articles in this thirty-year period, the *Social Science Index* and *Humanities Index* combined report 133 articles, and the *Index to Legal Periodicals*, a more difficult source to plumb, 150 articles. Taken together, 1,756 articles which professional indexes labeled or cross-referenced as dealing with child abuse were published in three decades, with the numbers growing steadily for each year after 1962.[28]

Each discipline had its own reasons for taking up the issue. For example, child abuse became an important legal issue as much because of legal interest in the children's rights movement as from the pressures put on the legal system by such medically induced concerns as temporary custody rules for abused children. The results were the same, regardless of profession. Medicine, law, education, social work, and the social sciences created a demand for scholarly research on how to define, treat, and prevent child abuse. The professions then set about to fill the demand they themselves created.

Child abuse even came to have its own journal, now called *Child Abuse and Neglect: The International Journal*. This journal, which is more an outlet for topical articles than a forum for weighty scientific discourse, was founded in 1976. Its editorial board looked like a *Who's Who* of pioneers in the field. Kempe was editor-in-chief, aided by such notables as Ray Helfer, Richard Gelles, and Joseph Goldstein.

The founding of this journal serves as a warning against ascribing all the growth of professional media coverage of child abuse solely to the moral imperative of the topic. The last two decades have witnessed an explosion of knowledge, unparalleled, perhaps, since the invention of the printing press. All the indexes that list articles on child abuse now reference many more journals than they did in

Annual Number of Citations

Cumulative Number of Citations

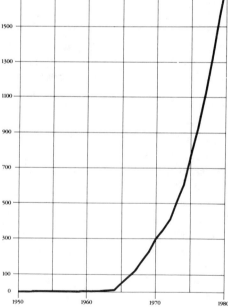

Figure 4.2. Sources: *Index Medicus, Education Index, Social Science Index, Humanities Index,* and the *Index to Legal Periodicals.*

1960. In 1980, *Index Medicus* covered 973 more journals than it did in 1960, and the other indexes now cover a larger number of journals as well.[29] One of the reasons that a new topic like child abuse could receive so much attention is that it did not squeeze out other topics with established constituencies. Quite simply, it was easier for child abuse to sustain extensive coverage because the number of outlets was growing. There were more slices of the publishing pie to go around because the pie was getting bigger.

The net increase in pages devoted to professional journals also allowed topic differentiation and issue aggregation to do their work in sustaining professional coverage. A quick scan of the titles of articles in, say, 1964 and 1979, shows how much the problem had been both specified and enlarged in fifteen years. In the *Education Index*, to examine just one source, the four articles mentioned in the 1964 volume were general in nature—profiles of abusers or victims, for example. In the 1979 volume of the *Index*, the forty-two articles cover a much wider range of topics, including articles on rural child abuse, child abuse as a cause of children running away from home, and numerous articles on prevention and intervention, to name just a few. In addition, the 1979 volume also includes the heading "child molesting," an indication of how, with the help of the anti-rape movement, the problem of child abuse has been separated into distinct, smaller problem areas, each receiving media attention through the same formula as child abuse.

Once child abuse and neglect were adopted as policy issues, public funds supported much of the research reported in professional journals. The Children's Bureau spent over a million dollars between 1962 and 1967, and $160 million was authorized (though not all was appropriated) under CAPTA and its reenactments through 1983. But public interest in child abuse was not limited to scientists and practitioners. The attention of the mass public was also engaged, quite deliberately in fact, by professionals who felt that government should take a greater responsibility for child protection. C. Henry Kempe certainly wanted the world to know the seriousness of the problem of physical abuse. One person who watched Kempe take his case to the press described him as having "the characteristics of crusaders, in the tradition of women reformers."

Newspaper Coverage

Newspaper accounts of abuse were extremely important in setting the government's and the citizenry's agendas. In the same year that "The Battered-Child Syndrome" was published, the Children's Division of the American Humane Association reviewed the major newspapers in forty-eight states to determine how many child abuse cases were reported by papers. They learned of 662 incidents, of which 178, or almost one-fourth, led to the death of the child. The study tells us nothing about the total number of cases of physical abuse nationwide, only how many were deemed newsworthy by local papers. But what had formerly appeared as isolated incidents of psychopathic behavior could now be understood as a patterned problem when over 600 cases were identified nationwide.[30]

The 662 abuse cases found by the AHA typified newspaper coverage early in the issue's life. During the early 1960s, child abuse was covered as crime news and the press found stories of bizarre brutalization especially newsworthy. But as time went on, newspaper coverage began to include—even be dominated by—stories reporting research findings. Of course, there could not be any reporting on research when there was no research to cover. But it is the *addition* of research-related stories which accounts for the durability of child abuse articles in the *New York Times*. Space for research-based stories on abuse became increasingly available as the *Times* editorial staff decided to give more space to human interest stories, especially those with a medical or scientific slant.[31]

The crime-and-victims approach to covering child abuse cases always assured a minimum of coverage for the issue. Reviewing research on newspaper coverage of crime, Joseph R. Dominick found that "a typical metropolitan paper probably devotes around 5–10% of its available space to crime news. Further, the type of crime most likely reported is individual crime accompanied by violence."[32] Thus, even if the media should tire of reporting other aspects of child abuse, child-abuse-as-crime coverage will remain. Indeed, it was always present at some level; it merely lacked a label to unify seemingly unrelated events.[33]

But child abuse reporting is not merely crime reporting: it is crime reporting with an important twist. There is a certain unfreshness about the act of abusing a child which adds a sense of personal and social deviance to the existing criminality. If a person robs a bank, it's a crime; but if a child is beaten, it's something more. One obvious motivation for emphasizing the most unusual and extreme forms of abuse is that newspapers can then titillate their readers with stories that are unwholesome as well as violent. The penny press of the nineteenth century and its twentieth-century descendents made no bones about seeking out just this type of story. "Respectable" newspapers, on the other hand, feel the need to cloak the decision to run such articles behind a cloud of scientific justifications. Adolph Ochs, who bought the *New York Times* in 1896, perfectly captured the nuances of this perspective: "When a tabloid prints it, that's smut. When the *Times* prints it, that's sociology."[34]

A close examination of four cases of child abuse at two different times when the public's agenda was first being set reveals a fascinating pattern of how this type of private violence becomes "public property." A certain number of American children have always been abused or neglected, but the press has exercised an interesting kind of discretion in deciding which incidents will receive wide coverage. In what might be considered a "natural experiment" I investigated newspaper coverage of four different cases of child abuse, two occurring around the time of the creation of the New York Society for the Prevention of Cruelty to Children, and two others occurring around the time New Jersey first passed its Physician Reporting Law. I hypothesized that the press was more interested in cases featuring "torture" than in straightforward murder cases. Like all natural experiments, not all the crucial variables could be controlled. Nonetheless, in the cases I examined the press consistently found instances involving blue-collar stepparents who engaged in the bizarre brutalization of a girl (where the girl managed to live through the ordeal) more newsworthy than instances when natural parents caused the death of a boy through severe abuse.

The first two cases occurred in 1873 and 1874. They involved John Fox, the thirteen-year-old son of Peter Fox and his wife (unnamed in the newspaper account), and Mary Ellen Wilson, the stepdaughter of Francis and Mary Connolly. On February 9, 1873, the *New York Times* reported John Fox's death, implying that it was caused by a terrible beating the boy received for "refusing to go after beer without the money to pay for it," even though Mrs. Fox initially claimed her son "died from injuries received from falling out the window. . . ."[35] A coroner's inquest was held on February 10; the jury found that "John Adam Fox came to his death by pleure-pneumonia, caused by injuries inflicted by [his father] Peter Fox." Peter Fox, an unskilled laborer of German origin, was then "committed to the Raymond Street jail to await the action of the Grand Jury."[36]

After this point, Peter Fox dropped out of the news. The *Times* decided not to report what became of him, if indeed the paper ever bothered to learn. For the *New York Times*, at least, such stories were unusual. John Fox's story is the only reported instance of cruelty to children covered in the *Times* in the two years preceding the Mary Ellen case, and indeed his story might never have made the paper had he not died from his beating.

Compare the coverage of the John Fox case to the Mary Ellen Wilson case. Mary Ellen, as previously stated, was beaten daily by her stepmother. Mary Ellen's family history reveals many of the conditions now known to signal a potentially abusive home. Mary Ellen was illegitimate. The child, obviously a source of family stress, was boarded out until she was eighteen months old. When that arrangement fell through, she became the charge of George Kellock, the Superintendent of the Out-Door Poor. Proposing a somewhat strange and archaic plan, Kellock released Mary Ellen to Mc-Cormack and his wife under an indenturelike arrangement which required that the child be taught that " 'there is a God,' what it is to lie, [and] instructed in 'the art and mystery of housekeeping.' "[37]

Additionally, Kellock required the McCormacks to report to the Commissioners of Charities and Correction once a year, an obligation they fulfilled only twice, although it appears they were never contacted by any official for failing to meet this requirement. Mary Ellen's father died, and her stepmother married Francis Connolly. At this point, Mary Ellen's stepmother began to beat her severely and the tale came to the attention of the *New York Times*. The *Times* followed the case for months, reporting the disposition of both the child and her stepmother (as well as an odd interlude when an Englishman presented himself as Mary Ellen's grandfather). The paper also noted that it was "the case of little Mary Ellen which led to the formation of the New York Society for the Prevention of Cruelty to Children"[38] as the *Times* launched into coverage of the New York SPCC itself.

With the formation of the New York SPCC, the *Times* began routinely to cover instances of cruelty to children, for the most part reporting cases which were known to the New York Society, suggesting that reporters regularly use the meetings and the minutes of the Society as a source of news. The coverage was intense and specific for three years, but became less frequent, but not disappearing, after 1877. The *Times* was amazingly eclectic in its child abuse stories, documenting children illegally employed as organ-grinders' assistants and street-circus performers, as well as more typical cases of neglect, abandonment, and physical abuse. The paper even reported abuse by adults in socially accepted positions of authority outside of the family. A police officer was chastised for using his billy club too freely and a teacher for viciously spanking a child in the classroom. Together, the articles made several interesting social statements. The accounts tended to have a distinctly anti-Italian flavor, but at this stage did not depict the typical abuser as an unnatural, unfeeling woman, as many recent articles have done.[39]

News coverage of child abuse cases during the consideration of the 1964 New Jersey Physicians Reporting Law parallels nineteenth-century coverage. New Jersey has no indexed newspapers, and the newspaper morgues for even large-circulation papers are unreliable. (The *Times*'s coverage of New Jersey is uneven at best, although it did publish brief accounts of the most notable child abuse cases and legislation in the last two decades.) However, since 1954 the New Jersey State Library has kept a clipping file on child welfare, and since 1967 has also maintained a separate file on child abuse. Not surprisingly, the files are more complete for recent years than for past decades, but because a large number of newspapers are clipped, it is possible to piece together an account of the Antonio Espinoza and Cheryl Ann Tabor cases in much the same way the papers' readers would have learned of them. The research on New Jersey media coverage of child abuse owes much to the work of several anonymous librarians who clearly had an interest in the topic. Of course, whatever biases or lapses in coverage these files contain cannot be assessed. However, because scores of papers were clipped daily, we can assume that few, if any, important abuse stories went totally unnoticed.[40]

As chapter 5 will show, the Physicians Reporting Law, enacted in the spring of 1964, was the first "modern" child abuse law passed in New Jersey. Two years earlier the legislature had also passed a bill reorganizing the State Board of Child Welfare into the Bureau of Children's Services. The law added or amended several sections of the State Code dealing with children's services. Thus child welfare issues were already on the legislature's agenda when the specific problem of child abuse was brought to its attention.

Unlike the massive, technical changes in the welfare laws, the Physicians Reporting Bill generated considerable interest in the press. By mid-1964 the papers safely assumed that readers wanted to learn about the bill because child abuse had already received considerable national media coverage. That fact, coupled with the prestige physicians bring to most issues they adopt, made the Physicians Reporting Law much more newsworthy in 1964 than were the 1962 changes in general statutes. But for all its newsworthiness, and all the space devoted to the legislature's activities, coverage of child abuse *cases* at this time still followed the nineteenth-century pattern.

The press's preference for reporting the bizarre brutalization of children, especially when it involved children of working-class parents, endured. On April 13, 1964, the day the New Jersey Assembly passed the Physicians Reporting Law, the *Trenton Evening Times* briefly reported the beating death of a two-year-old boy. The death had occurred a week before the *Trenton Evening Times* recounted it. The boy, not named in the article, was reported in other papers to be Antonio Espinoza:

> Last Thursday a badly beaten two-year old boy died in the emergency room of Paterson General Hospital ten minutes after the child was carried in by his father. . . .
> The father was charged with murder. Another child, an 11-month old girl, had bruises on her head. She was taken into protective custody at the Passaic County Children's Center.[41]

In several paragraphs the *Trenton Evening Times* dispensed with the story, which never reemerged in that paper.

Two weeks later a very different type of child abuse case made the papers. Once again coverage began on the day the legislature, this time the New Jersey Senate, passed the Physicians Reporting Law. Perhaps sensitized by the Assembly's passage of the bill, all the major New Jersey papers and the *Philadelphia Inquirer* gave enormous play to the story of Cheryl Ann Tabor. The similarities between Cheryl Ann Tabor and Mary Ellen Wilson are striking.

On April 16 a police officer came upon six-year-old Cheryl Ann Tabor wandering in a daze through the streets near her home. She was "found beaten and wearing a dog collar around her neck."[42] A police investigation later disclosed that Cheryl Ann was the "natural daughter" of Mary Stibitz and the stepchild of Charles Stibitz, a welder from West Deptford, New Jersey. Cheryl Ann's family history was not unlike Mary Ellen's. At the age of eight months, Cheryl Ann was made a ward of the state; but thereafter the newspaper accounts of her living arrangements became confused. At first it was reported that the child was placed in a foster home where "she remained for five years before entering West Jersey Hospital . . . [to test] the seriousness of a heart murmur. Then, inexplicably, she left the hospital in the custody of [her] natural mother."[43] Later reports amended the tale by saying that Cheryl Ann had been returned to her mother a year before her hospitalization because the court had decided that Mrs. Stibitz was no longer an unfit mother. The family was supposed to have been regularly evaluated by the Division of

Child Welfare, although in practice the monitoring was superficial and infrequent. Ironically, a week before Cheryl Ann's abuse came to the attention of the authorities, a caseworker had called at the Stibitz residence only to find no one at home.[44] The caseworker later testified to having made a mental note to return to the Stibitz home "as soon as possible."[45]

Like Mary Ellen Wilson's stepmother, Mary Stibitz was also convicted. Her court appearance must have been unusual in the extreme. She wore go-to-church clothes, a Jacqueline Kennedy-like dress, and a feathered hat, but broke from her demure role long enough to pose for smiling photographs in which she displayed the belt with which she admittedly had beaten her daughter.[46]

The cases of John Fox, Mary Ellen Wilson, Antonio Espinoza, and Cheryl Ann Tabor strongly suggest that the reporting of child abuse follows a fairly consistent pattern in which unwholesomely criminal cases where the child survives are preferred to what might be considered the more serious, but somehow more routine, cases where the child dies. The titillation of bizarre brutality accounts in part for this pattern, but other factors also contribute to newspapers' apparent preference for this type of story. Part of this preference can be traced to the organizational needs of newspapers. From the perspective of news managers, more information unfolds in a case of brutality than in one where the victim dies. This fact in itself sustains coverage.

But factors more subtle than an editor's bent for sensationalism are involved in sustaining newspaper coverage of child abuse stories. Most importantly, the press enjoys playing an advocative role in maintaining cultural norms that protect children and defend the integrity of the home. These expressions are part of the Progressive Era values sustained by the media in general.[47] Additionally, abuse which results in death is murder, or at least manslaughter. Society has clearly defined sanctions which are invoked in cases of murder. No similarly straightforward response existed for child abuse in 1964. Under the doctrine of "the best interest of the child," there was a presumption that a child ought to remain at home unless the situation was hopeless. With only limited temporary shelter facilities available and permanent placement options restricted to foster care or—what was even less likely—adoption, an abused child was frequently returned to his or her parents. The implicit difficulty in determining what was a safe environment for a child and the common-law precedent supporting strong parental rights together created a tension in bizarre brutalization cases which led to sustained coverage of these cases. The bizarre brutalization of young girls may also account for the newspapers' continuing interest.

In a 1965 nationwide public opinion survey conducted by David G. Gil, newspapers were cited more frequently than other media as a source of information on physical abuse: 72.0% of Gil's respondents mentioned newspapers as an information source, 56.2% specified television, and 22.7% cited magazines.[48] The newspapers' tradition of reporting child abuse as crimes of bizarre brutalization helps to explain why approximately 30% of Gil's sample felt that parents or other abusers should be "jailed or punished in some other way."[49] Indeed, with the extremely brutal images provided by reporting abuse as a crime, we may do well to wonder why over two-thirds of those queried preferred a more therapeutic approach to dealing with abusers, believing close supervision or even leaving the abuser alone if the injury was not too serious (or not intervening at all) to be a sufficient response. The message of "The Battered-Child Syndrome," which portrayed abuse as medical deviance, was clearly in accord with more general attitudes defining social problems involving violence as psychological in origin.

Once child abuse was rediscovered as a social problem, newspapers began to cover cases more frequently and intensively. But not all the growth in the coverage of child abuse was a result of papers' interest in bizarre brutalization. As legislative response to child abuse grew, so did that type of newspaper coverage. Every state passed a child abuse reporting law between 1963 and 1967, and all amended and reamended their law several times, with each legislative action renewing newspaper interest in the problem. In addition, newspapers also began to run human interest stories on child abuse, in part aided by the now defunct Women's News Service, which provided feature stories on child abuse for the home, style, and fashion pages of subscribing newspapers. Local human interest stories focused on nearby programs to prevent or treat abuse, and special training sessions for county and state workers.

In deciding to investigate or publish a particular story, journalists quickly learn that "hard" and "soft" news are not accorded the same value. "Hard news," according to Gaye Tuchman, "concerns important matters and soft news, interesting matters."[50] Soft news does not have the "quickening urgency" which Helen MacGill Hughes asserts is the lifeblood of newspapers.[51] In other words, soft news is timeless and durable—although many would say insignificant—which means it appears at the back of a newspaper.

The special titillation of violent deviance accounts for the durability of child abuse as soft news. Newspapers usually feature such news in the portions of the papers devoted to women's interests. These stories often dwell on the fact that most reported abusers are women, even while mentioning that this finding is not surprising since women traditionally bear the burden for most child care. The abuser is characterized as an "unnatural" woman, one who does not adequately love and protect children, and who finds child care less than totally rewarding. Human interest stories are frequently described as instances where a "man bites dog," not the reverse. What better fits the "man-bites-dog" category than the case of a mother who beats her child? The deviant aspect of child abuse cases lets the coverage glide easily into the category of soft-news coverage.

The role of human interest stories in sustaining newspaper coverage of child abuse can be seen by examining the *New York Times* stories in 1964 and again in 1979. The sixteen stories on child abuse published in 1964 split evenly between cases and legislative reports. Fifty child abuse stories made the *Times* in 1979. In that year the activities of various charitable groups and the results of numerous scientific research projects constituted *one-half* of the coverage. Cases, legislation, even criminal proceedings took a back seat to soft-news articles.

The pattern of newspaper coverage of abuse and neglect over the last thirty years is quite illuminating. Once again relying on the *New York Times Index*, we find that during the early 1950s child abuse stories were quite common, thinning to just a few stories a year until the late 1960s when coverage took a dramatic jump (see figure 4.3). The sheer volume of coverage is remarkable. Between 1950 and 1980 the *Times* published 652 articles pertaining to abuse, certainly enough to keep the issue in the public's eye.

Of course, the media can lead the public to water, so to speak, but cannot always make it drink. The information was available to anyone who wanted it, but how many people read which articles (or watched which televison programs) cannot be ascertained. And the information grew year by year, to an unprecedented volume, providing a climate of public awareness which initially encouraged elected officials to recognize the problem and ultimately caused them to maintain an interest in it.

In sum, we can say that child abuse achieved the public's agenda because the interest of a few pioneering researchers crossed the bridge to mass-circulation news outlets. Public interest was sustained and grew, however, because the media have both many *sources* of news and many *types* of audiences to whom they present the news. Through topic differentiation, issue aggregation, professional

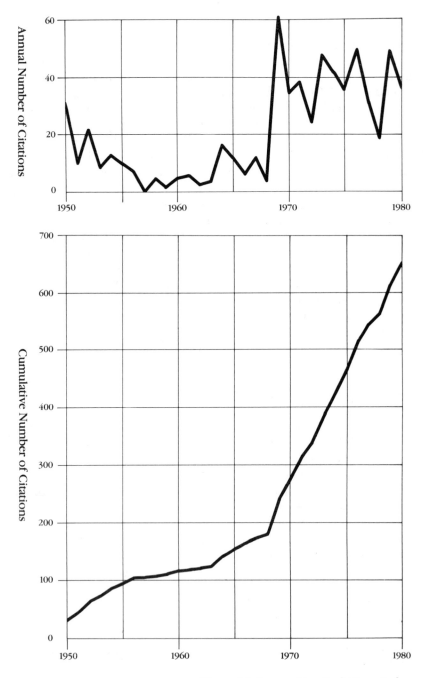

Figure 4.3. Source: *New York Times Index.*

and mass-circulation linkages, and the growth in human interest newspaper reporting, child abuse remains a lively topic of media coverage. The public's interest in this newly recognized social problem prompted state legislatures into action. And act they did, out of humanitarian interest to be sure, but also from the recognition that child abuse was the premier example of no-cost rectitude. The next chapter tells this story.

5. There Ought to Be a Law!

Between 1963 and 1967 every state and the District of Columbia passed some form of child abuse reporting law. These reporting laws diffused through the states at a speed five times faster than the average for public policy innovations between 1933 and 1966.[1] It is shortsighted and inaccurate to think of new issues of public policy solely in terms of legislation. In the case of the rediscovery of child abuse, however, reporting laws constituted the initial contemporary recognition of the problem at the state level. Only after the reporting laws generated an almost frenzied demand for services did states become concerned about meeting the demands they unwittingly created.

"Unwitting" is not too strong a word to use in discussing the initial state response to child abuse. In most cases, legislators acted from their hearts when they passed the first round of reporting laws. They considered the physical abuse of children disgusting, but few anticipated the relationship between reporting laws and the dramatic increase in demand for child protective services, indeed, for child welfare services of all kinds. Simply put, the legislators saw child abuse as a serious but not terribly prevalent problem.

But if the problem of child abuse did not seem important, the opportunity to be on the "side of the angels" did. Legislators also viewed child abuse reporting laws as an opportunity for no-cost rectitude. They were able to condemn violence against children at no cost to the public purse—only one of the original laws carried an appropriation with it. Certainly the symbolic character of the problem aided the rapid adoption of legislation in every state.

In this chapter we shall examine the rapid adoption of these laws more closely. That every state should learn about, consider, and pass child abuse reporting laws in only five years is atypical, to say the least. The first task, then, is to compare this accelerated diffusion pattern with other patterns of legislative adoption. Here we have an unusual opportunity to investigate the macropolitical forces promoting agenda setting at the state level. To this discussion we add a short case study of the passage of New Jersey's first abuse statute.

The case study allows us to examine the intra-institutional forces which drive the agenda-setting process. Finally, we shall consider the social consequences of these laws. Neither the welfare nor the legal system could absorb the demands brought about by increased reporting. Almost immediately child welfare agencies, juvenile courts, parents, and children were caught in the great conflict of values contained in the reporting legislation: whose interests—the parents', the child's, or the state's—does this legislation properly represent? Reporting legislation, which seemed utterly noncontroversial when originally passed, eventually became the field on which many bitter battles between the "public" and the "private" were fought.

Diffusion of Innovation

Child abuse reporting laws have been the subject of considerable research. Yet, despite hundreds of pages of commentary, very little of the analysis has considered the adoption of reporting statutes as an example of diffusion of innovation.[2] This omission is unfortunate because the rapid diffusion of these laws illuminates the process whereby child abuse as a private deviance is transformed into child abuse as a public policy issue. To chart this transformation we must answer four questions: What model of diffusion did this issue follow? What were the issue-specific "causes" of rapid adoption? Are there special characteristics of the venturesome (i.e., early-adopting) states which shed light on the speed of this diffusion? And what general social and institutional forces encouraged such rapid diffusion?

Models of Diffusion

What precisely is diffusion of innovation and what makes a state likely to adopt a new issue quickly or lag behind the majority of other states? Robert Eyestone, and Everett Rogers and F. Floyd Shoemaker provide the best answers. Eyestone succinctly defines diffusion as "any pattern of successive adoptions of a policy innovation,"[3] and an innovation, according to Rogers and Shoemaker, is "an idea, practice, or object perceived as new by an individual."[4] Eyestone then goes on to say that a "state's propensity to adopt a policy depends on three factors: some intrinsic properties of the policy, a state's politics and emulative (interaction) effects."[5]

The diffusion process can follow a number of different patterns. Most political research has emphasized the horizontal (state-to-state) links in diffusion of innovative state legislation. However, the case of child abuse is more properly classified as a modified version of point-source diffusion. In point-source diffusion the invention emanates from a single, often more powerful or hierarchically superior source and diffuses downward. In terms of political research, point-source diffusion investigates vertical relationships wherein states take their cues from the federal government.[6]

Point-source diffusion is often the product of the federal government's attempt to encourage a particular behavior at the state level. Most frequently, the states take their cue from a single piece of federal legislation which specifies how they should respond. The federal legislation usually provides incentives for state response, most typically the manipulation of access to funds. Of course, the states do not always say "How high?" when the federal government says "Jump!" Adoption of new policies by the states is often characterized by fits and starts, subject to local considerations.

Child abuse reporting laws can be categorized as a modified version of point-source diffusion. The Children's Bureau certainly provided the initial cue to states by promulgating its model statute. But this cue was not nearly as powerful an encouragement as, say, the Medicaid Amendment to the Social Security Act. Seen in a cold light, the Children's Bureau's model statute was simply a suggestion for legislation generated in a minor federal agency, a suggestion which had no binding power and thus provoked neither greed nor anxiety in its audience. But importantly, the CB's model statute was not the only cue the states were receiving. A number of organizations, including the American Academy of Pediatrics, the American Humane Association, and the Council of State Governments, were dissatisfied with the Bureau's model statute and proposed their own. Thus the CB offered the first and most "official" model statute, but not the only one.

State legislatures faced a barrage of model child abuse reporting laws in the years from 1963 to 1967.[7] In the main, the models differed only with regard to the person or agency required to report abuse. In 1963, the Children's Bureau recommended that reports of child abuse be made to peace officers on the principle that officers are always available. In the same year, the American Humane Association published legislative guidelines urging reporting to child welfare agencies, based on the principle that the law should emphasize the service outcomes of reporting, not the punitive ones, if reporting were to be encouraged. Then in 1965 the Council of State Governments published a model statute, a compromise between those of the CB and AHA, but which did support reporting to the police. Also in 1965, the American Medical Association, unhappy with guidelines that called for mandatory reporting under penalty of criminal prosecution applicable only to physicians, contributed its own model statute. The AMA proposed voluntary reporting by professional groups such as doctors, nurses, teachers, and social workers to either the police or a child welfare agency. The American Academy of Pediatrics devised still another model statute, published in 1966, favoring mandatory reporting only by physicians to social service agencies.

The role of these competing model statutes deserves more attention. Diffusion research, particularly on point-source diffusion, has largely been silent on the possibility of active competition among the models available to the states.[8] Of course, we can never know what the diffusion pattern would have been without competing models. State officials from New Jersey and New York, however, report that the competing model statutes (and mushrooming media coverage) superheated the demands for legislation. The parade of model statutes both encouraged rapid initial consideration of reporting laws and promoted reconsideration and amendments when the "most current" professional advice changed.

For these and other reasons, all fifty states adopted reporting laws within a space of only five years. Just how unusual this rapid diffusion is can be seen by comparing the adoption time span for child abuse reporting laws to other legislative innovations. In a study of scores of issues, Jack L. Walker found that the average speed of diffusion between 1930 and 1966 was 25.6 years, with the first twenty states adopting a given policy in an average of 18.4 years.[9]

Even considering that this time period spans many years when the pace of political life was slower than it is today, the contrast between Walker's findings and this diffusion pattern is striking. Moreover, the five-year diffusion of child abuse reporting laws occurred at a time when many state legislatures still met only every other year. For example, in 1963, 1965, and 1967 three state legislatures did not hold regular sessions, and in 1964 and 1966 twenty-seven legislatures did not call a regular session.[10] Thus most legislatures did not have five chances to respond, even though the diffusion of the initial round of child abuse statutes took five years. At best, a hefty majority of states (thirty) had only two or three opportunities to pass this legislation during the five years it took to diffuse.

Such rapid diffusion makes it difficult to analyze the case using the traditional formal model of adoption. Clearly there is little utility in trying to fit the standard S-curve to this diffusion pattern.[11] The problem with fitting the adoption pattern to the S-curve, is, of course, largely technical, created by the fact that all fifty states adopted the laws within five years (and more to the point, in three bienniums). The S-curve diffusion pattern usually shows a slow initial period of adoption, followed by a wave of rapid adoption, slowing down again as the last actors adopt the innovation. The persistence of the S-curve diffusion pattern over many types of innovation is believed to be a function of interaction (emulative) effects.[12] Communication among issue experts leading to a perceived performance gap is the most widely proposed motivation for emulation.[13]

Issue-Specific Causes of Rapid Diffusion

Experts on child health and welfare certainly talked to each other about the battered-child syndrome. As the next section shows, experts close to the Children's Bureau were instrumental in getting the states where they lived to pass child abuse reporting laws very quickly. But this elite network was not the only, nor even the primary, cause for this extraordinarily rapid diffusion of innovation. Rather, the symbolic and valence qualities of the issue, and the absence of monetary or political costs, better explain the rapid diffusion.

For the problem of child abuse, the valence nature of the issue is the most important factor in accounting for its rapid diffusion. Early laws focused mainly on extreme physical abuse, about which consensus was strongest and action appeared to be most necessary and warranted. Thus the issue maintained its valence character throughout the diffusion of the first round of laws. It was not until after states had several years of experience with reporting and service systems that the ambiguities and complexities of the problem became evident.

In the first round of legislation, only Illinois passed an appropriation to fund its reporting efforts. During this early period no other state felt that reporting child abuse would create the need for a new agency, extra personnel, or even special training for existing personnel, although such needs quickly surfaced after reporting began. Florida's experience is instructive on this point. In 1970, Florida authorities received seventeen reports of suspected child abuse. In 1971, the state began to take reports over a well-publicized hotline and the number of cases reported that year exploded to 19,120.[14] The child welfare agency could hardly process the cases let alone respond to them. Inevitably, that level of reporting generated demands for more money and personnel.

The nature of the issue, then, allowed legislators to be on the "side of the angels" without spending any money. The lure of no-cost rectitude motivated many legislators to act, and in the end, we must consider these individual motivations as a powerful explanation for the rapid diffusion of reporting laws. The need to appear publicly correct, decent, a person of probity and good will, is perhaps very much underestimated among the personal motivations given for supporting a particular political proposal. American political culture makes extraordinary demands on politicians in this respect, less so now in terms of their personal rather than professional lives. Divorce, for example, did not bar Ronald Reagan from capturing the presidential nomination, as it did for Nelson Rockefeller. But the demands to act ethically and to support the social and political values of the polity remain strong. Child abuse reporting laws played to these demands.

"Venturesome" States: Reasons For Early Adoption

Even in a very rapid diffusion process, some states must pass reporting laws before others. It is useful, then, to ask what differentiated "venturesome" states from their neighbors.[15] The answer is found in their predisposition to innovate. Many, but not all, of the states which passed reporting laws in 1963 (when the CB model statute was distributed) are venturesome in general. Their political cultures and institutional infrastructures support innovation, especially social welfare innovation. In addition, lobbying by people active in the early medical research and model law efforts also played a role in those states which were quick to pass reporting laws.

In 1963 ten states enacted "progressive" child abuse reporting laws: California, Colorado, Florida, Idaho, Minnesota, Ohio, Oregon, Pennsylvania, Wisconsin, and Wyoming. (In addition, Maryland, Indiana, and Oklahoma passed laws defining child abuse as a crime. These laws are not considered here.) Seven of the states are among the top quartile of innovative states as measured by Walker's composite innovation measure (California, Pennsylvania, Oregon, Colorado, Wisconsin, Ohio, and Minnesota). Walker's discussion of regional influences suggests why Florida was quick to pass this law. Florida is often touted as a regional innovator even though a number of Southern states have higher innovation scores.[16] So too Virgina Gray's research shows that Idaho, an early adopter of abuse laws, is a strong innovator on social welfare issues. All in all, the venturesome states were "doing what came naturally" when they climbed on the reporting bandwagon early.[17]

In addition, venturesome states were often home to venturesome people. It is no coincidence that many of the scholars active in child abuse research lived in states which first passed reporting laws. For example, Colorado, Ohio, and California were well represented in research and policy circles. Physicians like Dr. C. Henry Kempe (Colorado), his coauthor Dr. Frederic N. Silverman (Ohio), and their colleague Dr. John L. Gwinn (California) were very important in promoting public awareness and state action. Their personal efforts, their long-term commitment, and the fact that they were ready to act, helps to explain the "venturesomeness" of their states.

Social and Institutional Forces Supporting Rapid Diffusion

Too much emphasis on the specific example of child abuse or the characteristics of early-adopting states could blind us to the more general forces which also contributed to the rapid diffusion of reporting laws. In this period, state laws and state legislatures were undergoing important structural changes. Organizational theorist Lawrence Mohr suggests that "an organization may be more likely to innovate when its environment is rapidly changing than when it is steady. In this sense, 'environment' includes such factors as market conditions, technological changes, clientele needs and demands and the labor market."[18]

We can begin to understand the rapid adoption of child abuse reporting laws by transporting ourselves back to the "Camelot" of President John F. Kennedy. Many claims have been made for this era, particularly in terms of the "can-do" spirit of the times. The "best and the brightest" need only be assembled; a rational, well-thought-out plan formulated; and long-standing problems would fall to the blow of the lance.

One aspect of the reigning rationalism was the faith in legislation as a method of solving problems. This is seen in the use of legislation to attack such evils as discrimination in housing, public accommodation, and voting. It is also seen, however, in the legal profession's attempt to rationalize, modernize, overhaul, and update American statutory law through a two-decade effort in model statute writing. The American Law Institute (ALI) made notable efforts in the 1950s to formulate a Model Penal Code. The ALI met with less success in promulgating uniform state civil laws, although the standardization of commercial law between states made steady gains.

The reformers' cry, "There ought to be a law," was thus well received under the domed roofs of many state capitols.[19]

The institution of the state legislature underwent important changes as well. The capacity of state legislatures grew, more states met yearly, reapportionment lessened rural hegemony in state legislatures and brought urban concerns to the attention of lawmakers, and legislatures became "congressionalized" through full-time professional staffs and the creation of standing committees and subcommittees. Leadership, too, became more centered in institutional roles than in state political roles.

The legislators themselves changed. Formerly, legislators came from one of two molds. Some wanted to spend four to six years in the capitol and then return, with good connections, to their law practices or real estate offices. Others spent a lifetime as part-time legislators. Beginning in the 1960s that configuration began to erode. Younger men (but few women) with far-reaching political ambition began to populate state legislatures in growing numbers. The assemblies began to lose some of their amateur character as legislators began self-consciously to promote issues on the basis of their long-range political goals. These new legislators quickly learned the value of claiming an issue in which to develop expertise and on which to build name-recognition. The demand for new issues became so insatiable that Alan Rosenthal, a noted expert on state legislatures, reported having once received a frantic call from the senior aide of the Speaker of the House in a large industrial state who cried, "An issue, an issue. The Speaker needs a new issue!"[20] A child abuse reporting law was just such an issue.

Child Abuse Legislation in New Jersey

The full story of how child abuse reporting laws were passed requires examining the workings of state legislatures as well as a discussion of more general political trends. An initial examination of the records of every state legislature showed that the legislative histories of the original laws were remarkably similar. An in-depth examination of six states (which varied in terms of early or late adoption and propensity to innovate social welfare policy) showed no important differences in the political process or outcome. Thus, I chose my home state, New Jersey, as the location of my case study of the legislative process at the state level.

The 1964 Physicians Reporting Law was the first child abuse reporting statute in New Jersey. Its supporters acted from a variety of motives. Undoubtedly the lure of sponsoring legislation as popular and noncontroversial as this made legislators especially receptive when approached by physicians and social workers. But the appeal of no-cost rectitude must be understood in its larger context. State legislators had modest ambitions for the first reporting laws. The problem addressed by the law was not really abuse itself, but doctors' unwillingness to report abuse. Child abuse reporting laws belonged to the tradition of public health laws. No one anticipated that they would become a vehicle for expanding child welfare services.

As in most eastern states, the legacy of nineteenth-century interest in cruelty to children remained on the New Jersey statute books. Consequently a case study of child abuse legislation in New Jersey must extend from 1880, when the first anti-abuse law was passed, to the present, and include the numerous amendments to the 1964 legislation. In reconstructing this history the pressures on the contemporary legislation become clear, and we can see how reporting laws were transformed into social service laws whose goals were often social and economic justice as well as protecting individual children, and the physicians, reporting abuse.

In the nineteenth century, New Jersey, like many other states, passed anti-child-abuse legislation. In 1880 the legislature made abuse and neglect misdemeanors punishable by a fine of ten to fifty dollars and no more than six months' imprisonment. In 1883 the fine was raised to one hundred dollars.[21] Both laws prohibited children from being employed in certain "immoral"—though not particularly dangerous—occupations such as organ-grinders' assistants. The laws, like those passed in other states, remained silent on the matter of children working in factories or at sweated labor.

The New Jersey laws fell squarely within the poor law tradition, which supported the breakup of families for reasons of poverty. In essence, the anti-abuse laws explicitly added physicial abuse and moral danger to the reasons for removing children from their homes.[22] The end of the nineteenth century saw a change in this approach, however. Progressive reformers attempted to distinguish between destitution and neglect or abuse. The triumph of this view came during the 1909 White House Conference on Children, which disavowed family breakup because of poverty. The *Report* of the Conference was quite clear: "Children of parents of worthy character, suffering from temporary misfortune, and children of reasonable and efficient mothers, who are without the support of normal breadwinners, should as a rule be kept with their parents, such aid being given as may be necessary to maintain suitable homes for the rearing of children."[23]

By 1915, New Jersey accepted the Progressives' approach by statutorily separating neglect and abuse from destitution. In that year, a comprehensive child protection bill was passed defining in detail "abuse," "abandonment," "neglect," and "cruelty," and specifying many of the procedures to be followed in each case.[24] Somewhat earlier, the Children's Aid Society (of Newark) was reincorporated as the Society for the Prevention of Cruelty to Children.[25] Earlier still (in 1910), New Jersey had adopted its version of Mother's Aid, which gave cash grants to women of good character who were responsible for dependent children.[26]

One effect of the statutory separation of destitution, neglect, and abuse was to "psychologize" the two latter, removing them from their socioeconomic context. But both types of legislation received public support because both purported to reduce delinquency. Indeed, in the fallow period between the 1915 abuse legislation and the 1964 Physicians Reporting Law, abuse was discussed mostly as a cause of delinquency, that is, as an intermediate problem which had to be solved in order to remedy a larger one. In January, 1957, the New Jersey Juvenile Delinquency Study Commission used this perspective to call for a change in the state's child custody law. Witnesses at their hearings emphasized the need to change child abuse and neglect laws in order to battle delinquency. Specifically, they argued for a law that would allow a child to come into the custody of the state without his or her parents first being convicted of a crime.[27] Such statutory changes were not made then, however.

In the same year Claire R. Hancock undertook a study of "thirty-five of the fifty-six mothers who were in the Reformatory for Women" (at Clinton) on abuse-related charges. This study, funded by the U.S. Children's Bureau, reviewed the complaints made against the mothers and the disposition of their children. Hancock made a number of recommendations. Like the witnesses who appeared before the Juvenile Delinquency Study Commission, she proposed the passage of legislation separating the disposition of a child's case from the prosecution of the parents. She also called for a new approach to child services for neglected and abused children. Arguing that no one agency could meet the needs of such children, she advocated a coordinated system—"Community Centered Concern"—integrating public and private services. Her article in *The New Jersey Welfare Reporter* was unusual among the child abuse literature of the time in its strong emphasis on the societal causes of neglect.[28]

Hancock's article may have planted the seeds for statutory reform, but they bore no fruit. In 1964, when the Physicians Reporting

Law was passed, her approach was not mentioned at all. In fact, her interests were not reflected in the more general reform of child welfare services which the New Jersey legislature passed in 1962.[29]

The Physicians Reporting Law can be seen as a perfect example of special interest legislation. A group of New Jersey doctors aided by private child welfare specialists brought their demands for a bill to encourage reporting to the state legislature. The resulting legislation passed so effortlessly that it is almost superfluous to divide the events into issue recognition, adoption, setting priorities, and maintenance.

The champions of this legislation came exactly from the quarters one would expect: prominent physicians and child welfare advocates. The most notable supporter was Dr. Harold A. Murray, a pediatrician who chaired the Health, Mental Health, and Education Committee of the New Jersey Youth Commission, and was a former president of the Medical Society of New Jersey. Also testifying in favor of the bill were Leontine Young, author of one of the first books on abuse from a social-work perspective (*Wednesday's Children*),[30] and the then executive director of the Child Service Association of Newark; Jack Owen, executive vice-president and director of the New Jersey Hospital Association; and Dr. Cary-Belle Hele, a fellow of the American College of Radiology.

The New Jersey bill benefited from a national climate supportive of reporting legislation. Dr. Murray's testimony, especially, attested to the influence of the media outside New Jersey. Though he did not refer to the article itself, Murray spoke of the battered-child syndrome. Other witnesses also invoked the most current professional literature. Jack Owen credited the Children's Bureau with providing "the stimulus for this nationwide interest in child abuse." Both Murray and Young referred to the work of the American Humane Association, Murray to an estimate that 10,000 children a year are seriously abused in the United States, and Young to the Association's efforts to collect published reports of abuse cases from all over the country.[31]

There was no organized opposition to the bill although one witness spoke against it. In rather confused testimony, Mrs. Rita M. Parrott voiced concern that a doctor's charge of abuse against a parent might be so powerful a condemnation that it would "have the effect of making maybe innocent people almost guilty until they could prove their innocence."[32] Despite the efforts of a number of committee members and witnesses, Mrs. Parrott remained unconvinced of the desirability of the bill.

Mrs. Parrott's concerns were prescient in a way, anticipating future difficulties in determining what constituted abuse or neglect. But her concerns seemed ill-founded at the time and the Physicians Reporting Law passed easily. It conformed closely to the Children's Bureau's model statute, requiring physicians to report suspected abuse to county prosecutors who were themselves required to investigate the case fully. On the basis of the investigation, the prosecutor could file criminal charges or file a complaint with the Bureau of Children's Services. Almost immediately the requirement to involve prosecutors early in the proceedings caused serious problems for child welfare workers.

The ink was barely dry on the Physicians Reporting Law when the legislature began to add amendments. In the next sixteen years the act was amended eight times. In 1971 two important changes were made. The first change entailed a revision so that "any person" suspecting abuse had a positive responsibility to report it.[33] This change was consistent with a nationwide trend to enlarge the categories of people required to report abuse. The second change, however, was more important. The 1971 amendments changed the reporting procedure so that reports were made directly to the Bureau of Children's Services, not to county prosecutors. County prosecutors were deeply disturbed by the change and attempted unsuccessfully to have the law returned to its original form in 1975. In 1977, a compromise was reached which amended the law again, this time requiring the Division of Youth and Family Services (DYFS), as the old Bureau of Children's Services was restyled, to relay certain reports to prosecutors.[34]

The disagreement over who should receive reports of abuse was much more than a bureaucratic spat. It was emblematic of profound differences of opinion on how child abuse cases ought to be handled. Social workers felt that relaying reports to prosecutors undermined clients' confidence in them and encouraged parents to conceal abuse to the detriment of children and parents alike. Prosecutors reminded social workers that New Jersey law required that "any person" having knowledge of a misdemeanor report it to the proper authorities.[35] When prosecutors in Passaic and Bergen counties learned of two exceptionally severe cases from sources other than DYFS, the situation became explosive. They complained to Assistant Attorney General Anthony Del Tufo. Del Tufo called a meeting at which DYFS was represented by Deputy Commissioner of Human Services David Einhorn.

Del Tufo and Einhorn knew each other well, and through their commitment to solving the disagreement amicably, they were able to formulate guidelines which articulated when social workers would relay child abuse reports to prosecutors. Jointly drafted (over nine long months) and jointly announced, the guidelines were later codified in the 1977 amendments. In Einhorn's words, "it was the first and only time when prosecutors and social service people did something together. The very undertaking of a joint effort was unprecedented."

Less local controversy surrounded the enactment of other important amendments. In 1973, the law was changed to empower physicians and hospital directors to take suspected child abuse victims into protective custody.[36] In 1974, the Juvenile Court was given clear jurisdiction over child abuse and neglect proceedings, a provision which itself was amended in 1977 to apply only to noncriminal cases.[37] But if locally noncontroversial, these individual changes represented an almost total transformation of the original intent of the Physicians Reporting Law. No longer was the law a minor piece of legislation encouraging doctors to report physical abuse and protecting them when they made such reports in good faith. Instead, the law became the keystone in a changing child welfare service system, a keystone greatly pressured from all sides and often unable to bear the weight of the disagreements over the extent to which the state should intervene in the family.

Interpreting Child Abuse Legislation: The Limits of Legal Reform

The many changes in the New Jersey child abuse reporting statute might suggest that state reporting laws became more dissimilar over time. In point of fact, just the opposite occurred. Although state laws have become more complex, they have also become more similar. This convergence was driven by two forces. First, the federal legislation—CAPTA—required that reporting laws conform to ten dicta in order for states to be eligible for discretionary service monies.[38] Second, legal scholars, often but not always funded through CAPTA, undertook another round of efforts to devise comprehensive model reporting legislation.[39] Early in the second round of model statute writing, mainstream legal opinion supported the propriety of state intervention in abuse cases and encouraged the use of "protective custody" provisions which became prevalent in reporting statutes.[40] The objective of protective custody provisions was to give certain groups, mainly physicians and police officers but sometimes child welfare workers, a tool for protecting children from renewed abuse if they were returned to their caretakers. The problems of protective custody were readily acknowledged: temporary protective custody easily devolved into permanent custody, child welfare bureaucracies moved at a notoriously slow pace, and safe, noncoercive protective shelters were few and far between. But lawmakers felt that the principle of protecting children from immediate harm superceded both administrative and civil-libertarian concerns.

The protective custody provisions signaled an important change in the function of reporting laws. By including such provisions, the laws firmly connected strong, easily administered reporting systems to lumbering, conflict-ridden legal and welfare systems. Reporting legislation was no longer a blend of public-health do-goodism and malpractice insurance for physicians concerned about mistakenly labeling an injury as abuse. Instead, reporting legislation became child welfare legislation, subject to all the tensions over family autonomy, individual rights, and the role of the state that welfare legislation engenders.

The problem with protective custody came in cases of neglect rather than of physical abuse. Some states included "neglect" in their reporting statues in an attempt to have a strong, comprehensive law. Others did so without attention to the consequences, or out of habit, knowing that child protective legislation traditionally expressed a concern with neglect. Whatever the reasons, child welfare workers increasingly used the protective custody provisions to remove children from a wide range of harmful or potentially harmful situations. For instance, in New Jersey alone, 20,859 petitions for the temporary custody of children were made in 1979, 1200 of which were classified as "emotional neglect."[41] The welfare workers ought not to be faulted. Confronted with Solomon-like decisions about the safety of children, they often chose to err on the side of removing a child from a dangerous or difficult situation. A mistake in judgment, resulting in harm to a child, put workers in an extraordinarily difficult personal and professional situation. The extreme stress encountered by child protective workers is well documented.[42] Moreover, the stress encountered by child protective workers increased in comparison with other welfare workers (e.g., in AFDC offices), whose jobs became more clerical and routine in the 1970s.[43]

Without a doubt welfare workers used reporting laws as a tool to respond to inadequate family resources when comprehensive economic and social help was difficult to obtain. The public might be encouraged to believe that abuse was equally present everywhere, and always had the same meaning. But many child-care professionals saw this was not true. Abuse and neglect were often intimately connected with poverty, racism, and patriarchy. It was mostly welfare workers, however, who had to face this connection in their jobs.

Without intending it, the protective custody provisions of reporting laws reestablished the possibility of removing a child from his or her home for reasons of poverty. That possibility—indeed, that practice—had always existed, even after the Aid to Dependent Children program proclaimed a national policy of supporting poor children in their own homes. This possibility and practice, deriving from the fact that other more direct responses to poverty were largely unavailable, brought together an odd coalition of anti-interventionists, each urging that child abuse legislation refocus primarily or exclusively on physical abuse, thus limiting the use of protective custody and state intervention in families.

Three very different groups voiced anti-interventionist concerns. Liberal lawyers like Michael S. Wald of Stanford University expressed two types of reservations with an easy option to remove children from their homes. The first was that intervention had the effect of separating disproportionate numbers of poor and minority children from their families. The second reservation was that placing a child in foster care, the usual "solution" to abuse or neglect, was often substituting an unknown evil for a known one.[44] Moreover, a child placed in foster care is likely to remain there for a long time because parents or guardians do not lose permanent custody of their children. In 1980 an estimated 500,000 children were in foster care, almost half of them had been there for two years, and about 100,000 were six-year veterans of this "temporary" arrangement.[45]

Concern about the separation of children from their psychological parents added another group to anti-interventionist forces. Joseph Goldstein, Anna Freud, and Albert J. Solnit, authors of *Beyond the Best Interests of the Child* (1973) and *Before the Best Interests of the Child* (1979), argue for keeping children with their psychological (most often their biological) parents unless there is a "gross failure of parental care."[46] Theirs is the most extreme anti-interventionist argument to date. Using exceedingly narrow definitions, the authors would allow the state to intervene only in cases of abandonment, physical injury, sexual abuse, and failure to provide medical care. They give absolute primacy to the assertion that children need to believe that their "parents are omniscient and all-powerful" if proper psychological development is to occur.[47]

A host of legal and child development scholars have found the noninterventionism of *Before the Best Interests of the Child* excessive and insensitive to the realities of the legal and welfare systems.[48] But the authors' interest in authority patterns within the family is shared by the third group supporting limited state intervention. This group comprises conservatives who support traditional (patriarchal) power arrangements in the family. The Family Protection Act of 1981, sponsored by Senators Roger Jepsen (R., Iowa) and Senator Paul Laxalt (R., Nev.), typifies the views of this group. If the bill had passed, it would have reprivatized almost all interactions between parents and children—including physical "punishment"—thus making it difficult to define abuse and determine when it occurs.

Supporters of one group are often quite wary of the reasons other groups give for holding noninterventionist beliefs. The combined impact of their arguments has already been felt, however. Part of the movement toward less intervention in troubled families is pragmatic in origin. Legal scholar Stanley Z. Fisher says it well: "As resource starved state welfare agencies begin to grapple with the huge administrative burden of processing reports and as the federal aid carrot shrivels, we can expect more legislative restraint."[49]

Such restraint can be seen in the Supreme Court's majority opinion in *Santosky v. Kramer*, which held that clear and convincing evidence is necessary to terminate parental custody, a standard more rigorous than the "fair preponderance of evidence" required in the New York Family Court, where the original proceedings were held.[50] More than half the states already require clear and convincing evidence to terminate custody, so in that regard *Santosky* is consistent with current judicial practice. But a moderately high evidentiary hurdle clearly favors the parents' interests over the children's in child abuse cases. In itself, parental preference is not necessarily "wrong." American jurisprudence assumes that parents have positive responsibilities toward their children which are, in the main, adequately met because these parents are guided by "natural affection." The larger message of *Santosky*, however, is that the medical deviance model of abuse and neglect is still in play. Reporting laws originally constructed to encourage doctors to "protect" individual children from extreme physical abuse will continue to do so. But these laws cannot, perhaps should not, be used to address larger questions of equity and redistribution. Thus the movement toward less state intervention in abuse and neglect cases exemplifies the proper—and problematical—limits of legal, and liberal, reform.

6. Congress

As soon as they learned of the problem of child abuse, officials in the Children's Bureau and the state legislators placed the issue on their agendas. Special circumstances helped to compress the agenda-setting process in both these arenas. Issue recognition blended almost immediately into issue adoption in the Children's Bureau, largely because the problem was thought of as a specification of the Bureau's general child welfare role, rather than a new or competing role. Similarly, state legislatures moved rapidly from recognition to adoption because the problem was brought to their attention in tandem with a specific, limited solution: reporting laws.

The fact that recognition and adoption occurred virtually simultaneously in these two instances does not mean, however, that all agenda setting is so compressed. For example, ten years elapsed between the time Congress first denounced child abuse and the passage of national legislation. Interestingly, the problem of child abuse was first brought to the attention of Congress in 1964 when Representative Abraham J. Multer (D., N.Y.) introduced H.R. 9652, which would have required mandatory reporting of physical abuse in the District of Columbia. Another version of the bill was passed in 1966.

It is easy to understand why the issue did not move beyond the D.C. Committee. Service on the District of Columbia Committee is considered to be time spent in the Caucasus—nothing which promotes a member's career happens there.[1] Moreover, it was not at all clear just what Congress as a whole could or ought to do about the problem of child abuse and neglect. In terms of issue recognition, members of Congress usually follow the practice of old-time country doctors: they don't diagnose what they can't cure. In fact, even prescribing a cure does not assure issue adoption. For instance, in 1969, five years after the first D.C. child abuse reporting law was introduced, a number of bills calling for uniform national reporting procedures and extensive social services were introduced by Representative Mario Biaggi (D., N.Y.). No hearings were held on any of these bills and none was reported out of committee. It was not until 1973, when Senator Walter F. Mondale (D., Minn.) became interested in the problem of child abuse, that issue recognition progressed to issue adoption. Mondale—the liberal advocate of social programs—sponsored the bill, which after modifications became the Child Abuse Prevention and Treatment Act (CAPTA) of 1974.

Less than a decade later, Senator Jeremiah Denton (R., Ala.)—a conservative member of the Moral Majority and the chair of the Subcommittee on Aging, Family, and Human Service—almost allowed the problem of child abuse to lapse from specific congressional responsibility. Saved by last-minute horse trading, federal child abuse legislation was barely reauthorized by the Omnibus Reconciliation Act of 1981. Its future in an era of social service cutbacks and research consolidation seemed precarious at best. But in the summer of 1983 the legislation appeared to be safe again. Congress had before it two bills which would extend the legislation for four years, and knowledgeable observers felt the reauthorization was virtually assured.

This chapter details and analyzes the journey by which the issue of child abuse initially achieved the congressional agenda in 1973, and how, eight years later, it nearly died from the early budget cuts of the Reagan administration. Because we are focusing on one institution (as we did in the analysis of the Children's Bureau and the New Jersey state legislature), we can present a detailed account of the relation between the political actors and their organization. This approach complements the more macropolitical direction used in studying patterns of state legislation and media coverage. The extended time frame, coupled with the fact that Congress keeps more extensive records than any of the other institutions studied, offers a welcome opportunity to examine fully each stage in the agenda-setting process. But before recounting the history of congressional interest, we should discuss the issue basis of agenda setting and the factors promoting congressional innovation.

Studying Agenda Setting in Congress

The Issue Basis of Agenda Setting

Congressional interest in child abuse resulted in part from its valence character. The problem was successfully packaged, promoted, and ultimately perceived by most members of Congress as completely noncontroversial. Voting for CAPTA allowed all but the most socially conservative legislators a chance to be on the side of the angels, while still concentrating their legislative efforts on the more conflictual issues—such as Title XX and Supplemental Security Income—which dominated the social agenda at the time.[2] These conflictual issues were also new to the congressional agenda. It is important, therefore, to examine how the valence character of abuse in particular shaped the agenda-setting process, as well as to discuss policy innovation in Congress generally.

Institutional studies rarely make the distinction between valence and position issues, and scholarship on Congress is no exception. However, some research, notably by David Price, pursues a very useful parallel approach which focuses on the substance of issues and the configuration of interests surrounding them. Price proposes that issue areas can be defined in terms of their salience to the general public or more narrowly based client groups, and the level of conflict the issues engender. He reports that members of Congress have the strongest incentives to become involved in issues which have high salience to the general public but low perceived levels of group conflict. Price names health research as a good example of a high-salience, low-conflict issue area. Health care delivery problems, on the other hand, are classified as high-salience, high-conflict issues. In this area incentives for congressional involvement vary considerably from issue to issue.[3]

In actual practice, many, perhaps most, of the issues Price characterizes as having high public salience and low conflict are likely to be valence issues. The definitional requirement that a valence issue imply only one issue-position necessarily means that valence issues have low conflict. Further, I suggest that most of the valence issues that achieve the congressional agenda have high public salience as a result of the implied universality of the issue's value premises, as well as whatever urgency and immediacy individuals ascribe to the issue. In addition, many position issues may go through an initial "valence phase," when, through packaging or apparent content, the issue first provokes a single-position response. Subsequently, the legislative process (or some other factor) breaks down the consensus supporting the issue. Obviously, it is in the interest of politicians to emphasize to their constituents the valence qualities of the issues they favor, to appeal to widely held political values as the rationale for their actions, and to minimize the conflictual aspects of their favored concerns.

Congressional Innovation

Child abuse is clearly an issue on which Congress rather than the president initiated federal response. The propriety of congressional policy initiatives in this and other areas remains the subject of a long-standing debate, whose participants range from constitutional scholars with philosophical concerns to practical-minded governmental reformers. Textbooks frequently describe the post-World War II legislative process as one in which the " 'President proposes and Congress disposes.' "⁴ Such a portrayal dismays a sizable number of Congress-watchers who hold that the traditional relationship between the legislative and executive branches—with a strong legislature and weak executive—is both right and preferable. Yet, for all the ink spilled on discussing the proper roles of the executive and the legislature in policy initiation, very little is actually known about the overall pattern of federal policy initiation. Estimates of the proportion of legislation initiated by Congress for the late 1960s vary markedly: "Daniel Berman guessed that only one of twenty bills considered on Capitol Hill is an administrative measure, although he adds that these constitute the bulk of major legislation before Congress (*On Congress Assembled*, Macmillan, 1964, p. 20). Robert Bendener claimed that half the bills considered in Congress originate (are drafted) in the executive branch (*Obstacle Course on Capital Hill*, McGraw-Hill, 1964, p. 31). Lindblom estimates that 80 percent of bills enacted into law come from downtown (*The Policy Making Process*, Prentice-Hall, 1968, p. 68)."⁵

Though no one seems to agree on how often Congress initiates legislation, there is agreement on the individual and institutional characteristics which are conducive to legislative initiatives by Congress. The personal characteristic most associated with innovation in policy making is recognized expertise within a certain policy area. In fact, policy expertise is expected of legislators. As one representative I interviewed remarked, "Congressmen don't like it if you are all over the map with your interests."

Most members of Congress develop their substantive expertise as a result of their public careers, particularly their service on congressional committees, which are, of course, organized by subject area. Because the policy work of Congress occurs in substantive committees, it is not surprising that committee characteristics predominate among institutional variables affecting legislative initiatives. The most important institutional variable encouraging legislative initiatives is the power accrued by those who chair committees, a power which historically results from the seniority system, which in turn rests on the tradition of "safe" congressional seats. This triumvirate—formal leadership, seniority, and safe seats—combine to enhance the majority party's role in legislative initiatives.

Of course, institutional factors promoting legislative activism find different expression in the House and Senate. Most observers judge the Senate to be more conducive to policy entrepreneurship. In fact, Nelson W. Polsby went so far as to call the Senate a *"hothouse for significant policy innovation."*[6] The Senate's advantage stems from three sources. First, senators have more "leisure" to initiate legislation because of their six-year terms. Second, for almost twenty years the Senate contained a large plurality of liberals, whose vision of an active government encouraged policy innovation. Third, and most important, there are more subcommittees in the Senate than there are senators. In fact, by 1973, when the national child abuse legislation was considered, the Senate sported 143 subcommittees.[7] Of these three sources of innovation the latter two deserve particular attention. Together the plurality of liberals and the availability of leadership positions provided the structural basis for a wave of social legislation unmatched since the Great Depression.

In terms of the Senate's composition, the 1958 election marked the beginning of a startling change, a shift from a Senate dominated by conservatives of both parties to, in 1975, a Senate in which liberals commanded a 45% plurality.[8] Ironically, the tide began to turn on Senate liberals in the next Congress. In each of the next three elections (1976, 1978, and 1980) the Senate lost five moderate to liberal Democrats. Eric M. Uslaner accurately describes the dynamics of the change: "These are hard times for liberalism. While the American public is becoming more liberal on 'life-style' issues, the opposite trend is clear on questions of public expenditure, the typical bread-and-butter issues on which sub-presidential elections are contested."[9] In addition, Uslaner suggests that all the "position-taking" done by senators may make them more electorally vulnerable than representatives, who devote more energy to constituent service.

It was, in part, the expansion of the subcommittee system which afforded senators the opportunity for "position-taking." This expansion (which also occurred in the House) was part of a "democratization" of the Senate promoted by long-time Senate Majority Leader Mike Mansfield (D., Mont.). Chairing subcommitees gave senators multiple opportunities to play formal leadership roles.

Important policy consequences stemmed from these structural changes. The subcommittee explosion gave every senator a definable policy turf where legislative success could be readily claimed and proclaimed. Concomitantly, party discipline appeared to have eroded, perhaps because access to institutional rewards depended less on loyalty to party leaders and party-defined causes than it had previously, and also because the electorate became less partisan. Certainly the subcommittee explosion contributed to the increasingly "single-issue" nature of national legislation. But for the senators themselves, access to the visibility and power arising from chairing subcommittees has proven a definite advantage. All in all, the increase in Senate subcommittees brought senators closer to legislative heaven by affording them the opportunity to be workhorses and show horses at the same time.

The opportunity for initiating legislation is not limited to the Senate, however, even though the structure of that institution facilitates such efforts. Committees in both houses vary substantially in their receptivity to policy innovation, depending on the norms guiding committee activities and the style and preferences of the chair. Thus even newcomers to the House can make important contributions to innovative lawmaking if they know enough to request, and are fortunate enough to receive, assignments to committees which encourage legislative initiatives.

The importance of a committee's "legislative culture" in encouraging or discouraging policy initiatives cannot be overstressed. For example, the first national child abuse bills were written as amendments to the Social Security Act. These bills, like all Social Security amendments introduced in the House, were automatically referred to the Ways and Means Committee, which was utterly unsympathetic to the proposals. The legislative culture of the Committee denigrates individual policy initiatives, especially from nonmembers, and encourages intracommittee solidarity. (Representative Mario Biaggi, the bills' sponsor, was not a member of the Committee.) The power of these norms was caught by John Manley, who wrote that the Ways and Means Committee "operates with accommodation and consensus utmost in mind . . . [and] with a minimum of disruptive conflicts."[10] And if the committee-initiative (rather than member-initiative) norm were not sufficient to doom these early bills, Ways and Means was equally well known for its lack of sympathy toward social service legislation.

In contrast, the successful national child abuse bill was introduced by Senator Walter F. Mondale, the chair of the Subcommittee on Children and Youth (now the Subcommittee on Aging, Family, and Human Services). Not only did Mondale benefit from being king in his own realm, he also profited from the prolegislative, member-centered norms of the relevant full committee: the Committee on Labor and Public Welfare, now the Committee on Labor and Human Resources.[11] Representative Patricia Schroeder (D., Colo.) introduced the companion legislation to Mondale's bill. Assigned to the Subcommittee on Select Education of the Education and Labor Committee, the House proposal also benefited from a

97

supportive legislative culture. Speaking of the full committee, Richard F. Fenno, Jr., writes: "Education and Labor members come to their Committee to make good policy. They inhabit a distinctly pluralistic and partisan environment; and they happily operate as integral elements of party-led policy coalitions in that environment."[12] What a far cry from the regimented, highly centralized legislative culture of the Ways and Means Committee, where earlier House bills had been assigned and then utterly ignored.

Congressional Response to Child Abuse

Issue Recognition and Adoption

A revised version of Mondale's child abuse bill passed both houses largely because of his leadership and stature, which in turn rested on his institutional power base. But it was a long road from the District of Columbia child abuse reporting bill to the enactment of the Child Abuse Prevention and Treatment Act. A detailed account of the decade-long process provides important insight into the agenda-setting process generally.

We can examine the issue-recognition and issue-adoption stages in tandem. The history of congressional recognition of the problem of child abuse begins with the consideration and passage of the District of Columbia's child abuse reporting law in 1966. Congress, acting in its "city-council" role for the District, first considered a reporting law in 1964.[13] Representative Abraham J. Multer introduced legislation on January 16, 1964. His bill, which called for mandatory reporting of certain kinds of physical abuse, died in committee. The next year a similar bill introduced by Senator Alan Bible (D., Nev.) met with the same fate. After two false starts, Congress finally gave the District of Columbia a child abuse reporting law in 1966.

The interest of the House Committee on the District of Columbia in the issue of child abuse did not lead to a more general interest in the problem in either chamber. Indeed, the passage of the District's reporting law left no mark on Congress at all. At best, this legislation ought to be considered as congressional housekeeping, a responsibility devolving on the national legislature because of the special legal status of the District of Columbia.

That Congress first reacted to child abuse through the vehicle of the D.C. Committees points out a paradox in studying agenda setting. Strange as it sounds, Congress passed a law relating to child abuse when, so to speak, child abuse was *not* on its agenda. What happened, of course, is that the District Committees recognized the need to encourage the reporting of child abuse and then adopted the issue in relative isolation from other congressional concerns. Quite clearly the agendas of the District of Columbia Committees were largely separate from the agenda of Congress as a whole. Thus the issue did not catch the interest of other members and therefore did not become part of the general consciousness of the Congress as a whole. In fact, no member of Congress or staff person interviewed for this study even mentioned the existence of the D.C. reporting legislation, let alone identified this early congressional effort as important to his or her recognition of the problem.

Congress's general lack of interest is easily explained. In the years when the D.C. reporting law was considered (1964–1966) child abuse was just emerging as a darling of the new journalistic interest in "medicalized" deviance. Most of the people who would ultimately be instrumental in setting Congress's agenda did not report being particularly aware of the problem during this early period. More important, most of the eventual leaders on the issue were not yet members of Congress. Walter Mondale had just entered the Senate in 1964, having been appointed to the seat vacated by Hubert Humphrey who was elected vice-president. On the other side, Mario Biaggi was first elected to the House in 1968, and Patricia Schroeder in 1972. Only John Brademas (D., Ind.) was an incumbent at this time, and his role in passing the national child abuse legislation was more as a facilitator than as an initiator. But even if this ensemble had served together, it is not clear what tune Congress would have, or should have, played. Agenda setting requires both a question and an answer. Beyond establishing federal reporting legislation, a doubtful enterprise for civil liberties reasons, it was not at all clear what federal child abuse policy ought to look like.

In 1969, Biaggi became the first legislator who tried to get Congress as a whole to recognize the problem of child abuse. Elected to Congress in 1968 from New York's old Tenth Congressional District (at that time completely in the Bronx), Biaggi acted quickly on his long-time interest in child abuse.[14] Almost four months to the day after taking office, he introduced the National Child Abuse Act which provided "for the protection of children under 16 . . . who have had physical injury inflicted upon them," required mandatory reporting, and established a nationwide child-identification system based on the issuance of Social Security numbers to children at birth.[15] The legislation was framed as an amendment to the Social Security Act and was thus referred to the House Ways and Means Committee. As a newcomer to the House and an outsider to the

Ways and Means Committee, Biaggi may be considered institutionally naive for proposing an Amendment to the Social Security Act. Not surprisingly, his bill died in committee. Though institutionally naive, Biaggi possessed political savvy. He knew there was still a great deal of publicity value in sponsoring legislation which would not receive active consideration. Convinced of the importance of the problem, he continued to introduce child abuse legislation—twelve pieces in all—during the years between his first election to Congress in 1968 and the passage of the Child Abuse Prevention and Treatment Act in 1973.

Without the support of the Ways and Means Committee, Biaggi was unable to translate his personal recognition of the issue into institutional issue recognition and, ultimately, adoption. If Biaggi had been a member of Ways and Means, or if he had designed his legislation so that it came under the jurisdiction of another committee, he might have been able to convince his colleagues of the importance of the issue. He certainly had more professional experience in dealing with the problem than did most other members. Biaggi could have argued effectively for his legislation because he had actually seen cases of child abuse during his twenty-three years as a New York City police officer. Not surprisingly, he dates his personal interest in the problem to those years. His decision to act on that concern when elected to Congress was solidified, however, when he noted that a poll reported in the widely circulated and inflammatory *National Enquirer* ranked child abuse as one of the three most pressing national problems. Biaggi's interest in introducing legislation was further encouraged by discussions with the publisher of the *National Enquirer*, Generoso Pope, Jr., and child protection advocate Dr. Vincent Fontana of the New York Foundling Hospital, both Biaggi's friends.

While Biaggi's interest and attention helped to set the stage for congressional recognition of child abuse, it was Mondale's leadership which secured the issue's final recognition and ultimate adoption. As chair of the Senate Subcommittee on Children and Youth, Mondale had the institutional power base from which to mobilize the entire Congress. The subcommittee had been created at Mondale's request in February, 1971. The opportunities, and limitations, it provided Senator Mondale, are aptly described by Ellen Hoffman, who was one of his senior staff members on the committee:

To Mondale the Subcommittee seemed a logical step in advancing proposals made by the 1970 White House Conference on Children. Other Senate committees, however, had long ago staked out their legislative jurisdiction over such relevant issues as education, health, and child welfare. Hence it was understood from the beginning that the issues to be addressed by the new subcommittee would largely be those that had not yet been 'discovered' by other committees, or those on which joint action could be pursued.[16]

The subcommittee first officially recognized the problem of child abuse in 1972, when it published a book of readings, "Rights of Children, Part 1," the impetus for which reportedly came from constituent inquiries.[17] The problem was adopted for action in February, 1973, when the subcommittee's senior staff members Ellen Hoffman and A. Sidney Johnson III sent Mondale a memo outlining a number of children's problems and a variety of potential solutions. Mondale chose to sponsor legislation against child abuse.

It is impossible to know fully why Mondale chose to recognize, adopt, and promote legislation to combat child abuse at this particular time. The web of motivation for any political act, perhaps any public behavior, is simply too knotted to unravel completely. But despite the difficulty in probing it, we need to explore Mondale's motivation because without his interest and initiative Congress might never have passed child abuse legislation, or if it had, the shape of the legislation might have been very different.

Mondale's career, past interests and future ambitions alike, contributed to his awareness of the problem and to our understanding of his motivations. Specifically, Mondale had been the primary sponsor of the ill-fated Comprehensive Child Development Act (CCDA), legislation which would have greatly expanded children's services, particularly "developmental" day care. President Nixon's veto of the bill was a stunning blow to all its supporters, especially because the reasons the president gave for opposing the measure centered around the impropriety of federal action in support of out-of-home care for children. This argument had never been central in legislative debates. The language of the veto was chilling, with the president maintaining that "for the Federal Government to plunge headlong financially into supporting child development would commit the vast moral authority of the National Government to the side of communal approaches to child rearing over [and] against the family-centered approach."[18] The impact of the Nixon position was made even more real—and painful—because, as one person close to the effort recalled, "the Comprehensive Child Development Bill was one of the most heavily lobbied human services bills, but the public knew very little [about it], less than [for] most [other bills]. And after the veto, a poll in Philadelphia showed 75% *of the people believed Nixon."*

Both Mondale's support for the CCDA and the bill's ultimate demise are important to understanding the senator's willingness to champion federal child abuse legislation. Mondale's efforts on behalf of the CCCD and his service on the Labor and Public Welfare Committee (now the Labor and Human Resources Committee) strengthened his credentials as a serious partisan of human service issues, credentials which, for example, Biaggi did not have at that time. The sting of the president's veto left Senate liberals simultaneously angry at their rough treatment and aware of the hazards other human service legislation would face. Clearly, comprehensive service legislation on any topic would meet stiff opposition. Similarly, any single problem targeted for congressional action would face executive resistance to increasing the number of categorical (single-issue) service programs. It is no wonder then, that when choosing among legislative topics, Mondale selected a single and relatively noncontroversial issue. The strategic value of his choice is captured in the phrase most remembered of him during the legislative process: "Not even Richard Nixon is in favor of child abuse!"

But an interest in the problem and a finely honed sense of political realities are not the only elements of Mondale's motivation. Mondale wanted to be president, and even though "he never announced," as one of his associates often repeated, he was being as candidatelike in the spring of 1973 as a senator with presidential aspirations ought to be. Championing an "apple-pie" issue such as protecting children from abuse could only help him.

Out of this web of institutional position, commitment to the issue, and personal ambition came Mondale's decision to go forward with the hearings for the child abuse legislation. To use the language of agenda setting, Mondale turned his personal recognition and adoption of the issue into his subcommittee's priority, and ultimately Congress's priority. He brought the issue of child abuse to a new place on the congressional agenda. Never before had any child abuse bill made it to the crucial juncture where the *legislature* rather than the *sponsor* had to act. Certainly Biaggi's earlier bills never received serious committee attention, and the District of Columbia's reporting law was, for all intents and purposes, an act outside of institutional memory.

Indeed, these two earlier efforts reside in a particularly gray and amorphous place in the study of agenda setting. They were recognized and adopted by a few individuals (even acted on in the case of the D.C. reporting law), but never entered the political consciousness of that institution as a whole. For an issue to achieve an institutional agenda, it must invoke some sort of official institutional response, even if only to be rejected. What constitutes "active consideration," a term which implies some level of authoritative decision making, is best determined by examining the "pulse points" of any organization, the places where formal and informal decisions are made and where decisions, once made, can be translated into organizational awareness, if not action.

Once Mondale decided to proceed with legislation, as he did in response to his staff's memo, the child abuse issue had reached the first critical "pulse point" in the Senate. One immediately asks, What did the senator and the subcommittee do to transform interest into successful legislation? In other words, how did they transcend their personal interest to establish the issue's priority within Congress and promote and maintain that ever-widening interest long enough to complete the legislative circuit? The answers to these questions are found by tracing the legislative history of the Child Abuse Prevention and Treatment Act (CAPTA). In so doing, we see again that, whereas the recognition and adoption of a new issue may occur at a fairly symbolic level, issue prioritizing and maintenance depend on *concrete proposals*.

For an institution to consider an issue, there needs to be, at the very minimum, something formal to debate and discuss, and in the context of Congress, this is most usually a bill. In fact, the submission of a bill renders the rest of the legislative agenda-setting process fairly routine; the methods of setting priorities and maintaining initial interest in a bill are straightforward and widely known, including all the time-honored practices ranging from soliciting co-sponsors through "Dear Colleague" letters, to holding hearings, to the more subtle negotiations which precede moving a bill from one stage to another, say, from full committee to a floor vote. Of course, once a particular bill or group of related bills is introduced, the agenda-setting stage of the policy process begins to blend in with the option-generation or "recommendation" stage.[19] Once again, it becomes clear that the analytical boundaries we impose on the stages of the policy process to further our studies, of necessity understate the complexity and interrelatedness of the actions themselves. Our discussion of establishing the *priority* and *initial maintenance* of the child abuse issue must, then, rest on a description of the changes in the content of the legislation as it progressed through hearings in both houses and an informal conference procedure.

Setting Priorities: The Senate Acts

The Child Abuse Prevention Act, S.1191, was introduced on March 13, 1973. (It later was retitled the Child Abuse Prevention and Treatment Act at the suggestion of Professor David Gil of Brandeis University. This is the name by which the legislation is known.) The text was drafted mostly by Ellen Hoffman, who was influenced by the work of Dr. C. Henry Kempe, the Colorado physician whose 1962 article in the *Journal of the American Medical Association* set the stage for the new wave of interest in child abuse and neglect. As Hoffman later wrote, this first version had four main points:

1. A National Center on Child Abuse and Neglect was created within HEW. The Center was to compile a 'listing of accidents involving children,' publish a summary of research on child abuse and neglect, develop an information clearing house, and compile and publish training materials.

2. A program of grants and contracts was established for demonstration projects 'designed to prevent, identify, and treat child abuse and neglect.' The amount of $10 million was to be authorized for fiscal year 1973, and $20 million for each of the succeeding four years.

3. A National Commission on Child Abuse and Neglect was created, consisting primarily of citizens outside the government, to study the effectiveness of existing child abuse and neglect reporting laws and 'the proper role of the federal government' in assisting state and local public and private efforts in the field.

4. In order to continue to receive funds under certain parts of the Social Security Act, states were required to adopt procedures for the prevention, identification, and treatment of child abuse, to collect information and report to the Secretary of HEW on the adequacy of state laws; and to make cooperative arrangements with state health education and other appropriate agencies to assure coordination in dealing with child abuse and neglect cases.[20]

Hearings on S.1191 were held for four days (March 26, 27, 31, and April 24) in three cities: Washington, Denver, and New York. They were designed, as Hoffman said dryly, to show the "human side of child abuse," in other words, to make the case for action compelling and unambiguous. The hearings included the testimony of a wide range of experts, several of whom showed colored slides depicting cases of brutality, extreme neglect, even malnutrition. In a politically sophisticated move the staff also arranged for subcommittee members to tour hospitals or other treatment programs as an indication that the problem was not without some workable solutions.

The staff did its best to present the case against child abuse in the most graphic way. Their task was made easier because neither incompatible economic preferences nor clashing moral opinions cluttered the consideration of the issue. Doctors and hospitals were the only groups or institutions which might have voiced an economic objection to this type of legislation, but there was really nothing much in the bill that affected them financially. Likewise, child abuse appeared not to harbor the conflicting moral assumptions present in, for example, the mine safety issue, where mine owners could talk about jobs and economic development, and mine workers could appeal to the value of human life and the dignity due labor.

One witness in particular captured the essential valence quality of the issue. She was Jolly K., a former child abuser and founder of Parents Anonymous. The senators were greatly impressed by her frankness and her powerful description of her actions, in which she stated that she knew she was hurting her child, and wanted to stop, but could find no help from any public agency to which she turned. "Did you abuse your child?" asked Senator Mondale. "Yes," responded Jolly K., "I did; to the point of almost causing death several times. . . ."[21]

In Jolly K. the subcommittee found a gripping witness, a figurative example of both sin and redemption, with sin being child abuse, compounded to some extent by the lack of public response, and redemption being the range of demonstration programs which might be funded under the bill, including, by inference, some assistance to struggling private programs such as Parents Anonymous. The senators were very solicitous of her feelings and thanked her quite tenderly for being willing to make public her story of "private" violence. "Thank you," said Mondale, "for . . . being willing to be embarrassed to help us understand a very great problem."[22]

As it turned out, the members of the subcommittee did not know the half of Jolly K.'s story, or how tragic yet typical her story was. She told them that she herself had been beaten as a child, in much the same manner as she had beaten her daughter. She did not disclose, however, a childhood scarred by abandonment, rape, foster homes, juvenile halls, and repeated delinquency, and a young womanhood of drifting, prostitution, bad marriages, and attempted suicide. For the subcommittee, there was only one "sin," (abuse) and one "redemption" (governmental response to the problem).[23]

However compelling Jolly K.'s story was, it would be wrong to assume that the issue of child abuse, though less conflictual than most issues, generated no conflict at all. Like most valence issues, child abuse lost some of its valence quality when examined closely. During the course of the hearings, it became clear that both the definition of the problem and the solution preferred by Senator Mondale did contain some elements of conflict which would have to be managed, packaged, diffused, or set aside to insure the bill's success.

Four important conflicts arose in the consideration of S.1191 by the Subcommittee on Children and Youth. Two were conflicts over the content of the policy, namely, whether to focus more on abuse than neglect, and how to establish the problem of child abuse as one which knew no class boundaries. The other two were the kinds of conflicts one would expect to arise when government really does take on a new issue of this sort. These agenda-setting conflicts included the debate over the proper role of the state in the upbringing of children and arguments as to whether new issues or programs ought to be housed in categorical or comprehensive legislation.

The first policy-centered debate focused on whether the bill should emphasize child abuse, child neglect, or both, and in what proportions. As Hoffman later said, the intent of the legislation, and by inference, the intent of Senator Mondale, was "that priority be given to helping children who are the victims of physical abuse."[24] The remarks of witnesses like John T. Allen, chairman of the American Academy of Pediatrics' Subcommittee on Child Abuse, supported this view. "I think," said Dr. Allen, "what we are really talking about, whether we want to admit it or not, is . . . the physically abused child. This is what we have got to focus in on." Senator Mondale quickly agreed. "I am glad you made that point. Unless you do that, you get into the question of sort of basic social health, which is beyond the reach of legislation that we can possibly do."[25]

Mondale's concern was to prevent the "best" from driving out the "good." The senator clearly worried that one or another vision of the "best" legislation—with a focus on a wide range of child welfare and development problems—would weaken the legislative prospects for passing what he strongly believed was "good"—though more modest—child abuse legislation. Not all the witnesses were pleased or content with his focus; they felt that milder forms of abuse, and certainly neglect, were very much more prevalent and therefore deserved more attention. Social workers and lawyers—as opposed to doctors—recognized that the creation of legislation and subsequent funding of programs against child abuse would raise unwarranted expectations that neglect would be addressed as well. Sooner or later, Congress would pay the price for favoring child abuse over neglect. Dr. Vincent De Francis, the long-time director of the Children's Division of the American Humane Association, argued this less popular view:

> We are concerned about the abused child, but children are abused in many ways, not purely the battered child, we have children who are sexually abused, we have children who are neglected in a host of ways. If we are going to address ourselves to the problems of children who need help we must address ourselves to the entire problem.[26]

Mondale was able to ride herd on the conflict between the "best" and the "good" by constant appeals to the reality of the legislative situation. To his mind the real stumbling block to passing the legislation would occur if it were considered poverty legislation, or if the problem were defined as a deviance confined solely to the poor, rather than as a social blight which attacked all classes. Over and over again, Mondale used his leadership position to emphasize that child abuse was a social problem which did not ignore the wealthy or middle class. On the first day of hearings, while questioning the very first witness (Professor David Gil), Senator Mondale asked, "Would you not say that the incidence of child abuse is found as well in the families of middle class parents?" Gil responded yes to that and to the subsequent question about upper-income parents. Mondale continued to press Gil, asking whether "this is a national phenomenon that is not limited to the very poor?" "Definitely so," responded Gil for the third time. But then the Brandeis professor added—somewhat to Mondale's discomfiture—"However, as I have said on another occasion, the factors that lead to abuse among the well-to-do are the same that also lead to abuse among the poor. The poor have, in addition, many more factors." Mondale quickly responded, "I know you are going to get to that. But this is not a poverty problem it is a national problem." Gil acceded with "That is correct," and the subject changed.[27]

Actually, neither of these substantive concerns—relative emphasis on abuse or neglect and the class character of the problem—created much of a stir outside the relevant committees in both houses, perhaps because Mondale nipped in the bud any serious objections on these grounds. With the aid of 20-20 hindsight, the conflicts over the proper role of governmental intervention in the family and the best location for programs proved more durable. They now form the basis of the controversy over this and other social legislation.

By emphasizing gross physical abuse over less visible forms of maltreatment, Mondale also deflected another set of conflicts, those centering around the proper role of the state in the upbringing of children. This conflict emerged not so much as a question over the extent to which the state can intervene to protect children from abuse (as the debate is now framed), but in two more subtle ways. To retain its valence quality, child abuse had to be dissociated from the discussion of a parent's "right" physically to discipline a child, a "right" which Congress would no doubt have supported if pressed. A certain unease over this issue can be noted in Senator Robert T. Stafford's (R., Vt.) remarks at the hearings. (Stafford was a member of the Subcommittee on Children and Youth.) In a prepared statement the senator wrote, "It is important to provide the means to help those parents who perpetuate abuse beyond what would be called '*normal discipline.*'"[28]

On this topic, as in the case of the conflict over the focus on abuse over neglect, Professor Gil's comments are noteworthy. He and Senator Jennings Randolph (D., W. Va.)—a member of the subcommittee—engaged in a long and spirited discussion on the question of whether corporal punishment constituted child abuse. The senator argued against such a "namby-pamby" notion while Gil continued to assert that "any use of physical force, and paddling, is in [his] view unacceptable."[29] Interestingly, whereas Gil thought that the government was not intervening forcefully enough in the problems pertaining to raising children, the opposite view was voiced in the House proceedings. When the bill was reported out of the Committee on Education and Labor, it contained the dissenting statement of Congressman Earl F. Landgrebe (R., Ind.). Opposing the legislation, he asserted that "to give the government total unconditional authority to prescribe regulations empowering the state to take children away from parents may be characteristic of a totalitarian state such as Nazi Germany or Soviet Russia. It certainly has no place in the United States of America."[30]

In this first legislative effort, these philosophical concerns did not actually "jeopardize" the passage of child abuse legislation, whereas the administration's opposition to the creation of another categorical program did have significant impact, even if "jeopardy" is too strong a word to characterize its effects. The reasons the administration gave for opposing Mondale's child abuse legislation are interesting. In general, the Nixon White House was opposed to the creation of any new categorical programs addressing social problems. In fact, the White House did not want to be bothered by consideration of individual social programs at all because the administration was trying to come to grips with the unprecedented rise in total social service spending which had occurred since Nixon's first term as president.

The result of the administration's efforts in this regard was the passage in 1974 of Title XX of the Social Security Act, which reorganized and, more importantly, also capped previously open-ended federal social services spending. From fiscal year 1969 to fiscal year 1972, federal expenditures for social service grants swelled from $354 million to $1.69 billion.[31] The increase resulted from a number of factors, including formal and informal changes in the administrative policies which encouraged states to spend more in this policy area. Specifically, the states were remunerated for the federal portion of these programs on a demand basis, that is to say, the federal government was required to pay the states the entire federal portion of the expenditures, regardless of the total amount spent every year. Title XX was designed to end this practice by regularizing and limiting the federal burden for social services. It was obvious that the administration did not care to support another categorical program, like Mondale's child abuse bill, when this problem would certainly be discussed as part of a comprehensive and "fiscally responsible" social services package. Paralleling the administration's view, some child welfare charities, notably the Child Welfare League, felt their efforts were better spent getting child abuse included as a designated service priority in Title XX than on passing limited child abuse legislation. This preference was fueled by a feeling that Mondale had slighted the League and the social-work perspective in CAPTA.

Even Senate liberals decried the consequences of an endless stream of single-issue social legislation, knowing that the programs suffered from a lack of coordination which not only ultimately diminished their effectiveness for the intended recipients, but also contributed to the public's sense of growing governmental ineptitude in dealing with poverty and social dislocation. Nonetheless, during the second Nixon term, in the period just before Watergate dominated the national consciousness, ambitious and legislatively sophisticated senators like Mondale continued on strategic grounds to support single-issue social legislation.

The administration repeatedly voiced its general opposition to new categorical programs through the testimony of various witnesses. Stephan Kurzman, Assistant Secretary for Legislation in

HEW, was the administration's principal standard-bearer at the hearings, where, for example, he told Mondale that "we would prefer not to try to split up the statutes relating to this [problem] into further boxes."[32] Kurzman also voiced the administration's Republican orthodoxy, saying that "basically, the Federal Government aids States and localities in carrying out their responsibility for the protection of children."[33] To shore up the administration's general opposition to the bill, HEW witnesses, led by Kurzman, also contended that the federal government was actually spending a significant amount of money on child abuse and child-abuse-related services. Kurzman testified that, as best the figures could be disaggregated, roughly $224 million of Title IV-A funds alone would have been spent between fiscal years 1971–74 on "protective services such as the immediate intervention and support necessary to prevent continued abuse or neglect of children,"[34] and that various other titles, agencies, and programs were funding services, research, and demonstration projects more or less directly related to the problem.

Mondale remained totally unconvinced. In the course of very pointed questioning he challenged Kurzman and the other administration witnesses to show precisely how much money was being spent specifically on child abuse and whether state response to the problem was both good and adequate. Repeatedly the witnesses found themselves in the unenviable position of admitting that they did not know the answers to the monetary or programmatic questions, but were, in Kurzman's words, trying to "improve our knowledge."[35]

Many of the permanent staff of the affected parts of HEW found the whole experience with the child abuse legislation painful and frustrating. Not only were they required to oppose publicly legislation which many favored privately, they were also old hands at this type of legislation and knew that *some* sort of bill would ultimately pass, even though the administration opposed it. One HEW official put it well, saying that he resented "being tainted by the Administration's position," especially because it soured relations with the Senate staff.

Another official felt the conflict between the administration's position and his personal views so keenly that it prompted him to resign. Dr. Frederick Green, the Associate Director of the Children's Bureau, was orginally scheduled to testify against the bill. Green, however, supported the bill and made known his uneasiness about being an opposition witness. Originally it seemed that Green would have to testify against the dictates of his conscience. At the last minute, though, another witness was designated, in recognition of the seriousness of Green's misgivings. However, because Green was still subject to congressional subpoena, he was "advised" to be sure to be out of town during the hearings. Green went to New York, where he spent the afternoon in the New York City Public Library. He knew he had reached a crisis in his public career, with resignation being the price of his disagreement with the administration. He wrote the necessary letter on the plane back to Washington that day. After presenting his resignation, Green was asked to make it effective after the debate on the legislation was over, so as not to have an untoward effect on its consideration. He agreed, and asked to make his resignation effective June 11—the anniversary of his two years of service in the Children's Bureau.

The tension many issue specialists felt between their professional judgments and competing claims for institutional loyalty illuminates another aspect of valence issues. In general, valence issues promote harmony within government; they emphasize a broad, almost natural, consensus in institutions which by definition spend most of their time brokering conflicting claims and divergent opinions. But for a valence issue to provide a respite from political divisiveness, it must be consensual within the framework of an organization's activities, as well as in terms of the implicit problem and solution the valence issue calls to mind. Thus, for many of the human services professionals in various cubbyholes in HEW, child abuse did not appear to provide quite the same opportunity to act righteously in the public interest as it did for most members of Congress.

It is a testimony to the perceived valence character of the legislation and the lingering belief in the efficacy of legislative solutions to social problems, that such conflicts were deflected during the Senate hearings. The final tally reflected the absence of serious conflict. The bill came to a vote on Saturday, July 14. Senator Randolph stepped in as floor manager because Mondale was "unavoidably" out of town, and everything went swiftly and smoothly.[36] Senator Jacob Javits (R., N.Y.,) the ranking minority member of the full committee, spoke early in the debate, showing his considerable legislative skill. In his peroration he managed to juggle a variety of seemingly conflicting views. He noted the administration's opposition, but supported the legislation, arguing circularly that the bill actually did what the administration wanted done. All of this was delivered quite gracefully and politely. Javits's support was not surprising; it would have been unusual for this social-policy liberal, even though a Republican, to oppose a bill like S.1191, especially when the price tag seemed reasonable. Moreover, the subcommittee showed a sensitivity to the political climate by holding hearings in New York City, which could not but please Javits, as they provided an opportunity for many of his constituents to speak. Senator Robert T. Stafford, a Republican of Vermont and a member of the subcommittee, also lent his unqualified support to the bill. Of these two Republican supporters, only Stafford remained in the Senate when the child abuse legislation came up for its second reenactment in 1981, and he was no longer a member of the subcommittee.

Indeed, it was a third Republican senator, Charles Mathias of Maryland, who offered the only floor amendment to the bill. His amendment, which not surprisingly had been discussed by the subcommittee prior to its being offered on the floor, required ("authorized and directed") the secretary of HEW "to prepare and submit annually to the President and to the Congress a report on the programs assisted under this section, together with an evaluation of such programs."[37] This floor amendment was added to several committee changes. "Language was added to emphasize the Committee's belief that multi-disciplinary programs were particularly worthy of support, and to require HEW to distribute the demonstration funds equitably among geographical areas and between urban and rural areas. In addition the requirement that HEW compile a 'listing of accidents' involving children (an attempt to move toward a national reporting system) was removed because of the civil liberties problems it might raise."[38]

This slightly modified bill received the overwhelming support of the Senate, with fifty-seven yes votes and only seven "nays." All the negative votes came from Republicans. Only one person spoke against the bill, Senator Jesse Helms (R., N.C.). His objections centered on the belief that legislation like this tended unwarrantedly to centralize power in the federal government. "I realize," said Helms, "that a vote against this measure will be misinterpreted by some as an indication of disinterest in the tragic problem of child abuse . . . [but] sometimes we must cast difficult votes . . . I pledged when I came to Washington that I would try to be consistent—that I would cast every vote to preserve the rights, and the responsibilities of the States. Thus, tempting as it is to vote in favor of this measure, I am compelled to vote against it."[39]

Initial Maintenance: The House Acts

Four months later the House took up the question of abuse in the Select Subcommittee on Education (of the Committee on Education and Labor), chaired by Representative John Brademas, a long-time friend of liberal social policy. The hearings, held in Washington on October 1 and 5 and November 12, and in New York on November 2, centered around three child abuse prevention bills. Representative Patricia Schroeder (D., Colo.) introduced the companion bill (H.R. 6379) to Mondale's legislation. Schroeder's legislation did not include the last, somewhat problematic title of Mondale's bill, which linked a state's efforts in responding to child abuse with eligibility for certain funds available through the Social Security Act. Representative Mario Biaggi introduced his own bill (H.R. 10552) which, unlike some of his earlier ones, sought to amend the Elementary and Secondary Education Act of 1965 rather than the Social Security Act. Finally, Representative Peter Peyser (then R., N.Y.; he later became a Democrat) introduced a third bill (H.R. 10968). The bills differed on whether they included a definition of child abuse, called for a blue ribbon study commission or national center coordinating federal activity, required each state to submit an anti-abuse battle plan, or mandated a central registry for reporting cases. These were substantive conflicts, which had been avoided in the Senate because Mondale's subcommittee considered only his bill.

Had the issue of child abuse been more controversial, the assignment of the House bills to the Select Education Subcommittee would have been a bad omen. Of the sponsors, only Peyser sat on the subcommittee, although Biaggi was a member of the full committee. Schroeder, who was widely and properly indentified as the "real" sponsor of House child abuse legislation, was not a member of either the subcommittee or the full committee. In addition, Schroeder was a first-term representative. She had been in the House for only three months when she began to champion child abuse legislation. It was unusual that she should get so much attention as the sponsor of legislation outside her committee assignments. Such activism appeared publicity-oriented to some of her colleagues and thus a violation of the norms for novice members. Not every member of the Select Education Subcommittee was pleased with her role. But in the end, Schroeder, Brademas, Biaggi, and Peyser crafted a bill which ultimately the administration did not oppose.[40]

The House hearings were less organized and single-minded than the Senate hearings. A large number of witnesses trooped through, touting the seriousness of the problem and trying to convince the legislators of the complexity of the problem, a message which had been unpopular in the Senate hearings. William G. Lunsford, the director of the Child Welfare League of America's Washington office, testified with some prescience about the pitfalls of taking a simple stop-beating-your-child approach to the problem:

> There exists among those deeply involved in preventing
> and treating instances of child abuse, a difference of opinion
> as to where the focal point should be, and the best method
> to be used. . . .
>
> For purposes of discussion, I have grouped the basic
> views under the headings "Medical View" and "Child Wel-
> fare Services View." The two points of view may be seen as
> the victim as patient versus social problems as patient.
>
> As I see it, the medical view is focused on the physically
> abused child. The central problem is seen as physical
> abuse, the battered child syndrome and what one does
> about it. The concern is not a global one, physical abuse of
> children is basically seen as a medical problem, *subject to
> individual treatment. . . .*
>
> The child welfare services viewpoint holds government,
> and the general community, as well as the parents or guardi-
> ans of a child, responsible for the child's upbringing. Gov-
> ernmental responsibility is recognized in the laws relating
> to neglect and abuse, the ability of the courts to terminate
> parental rights, et cetera. The child welfare services view-
> point does not separate physical abuse from neglect, sexual
> abuse, or exploitation. The child welfare services viewpoint
> seeks preemptive action in the form of services. . . .[41]

To give more emphasis to child welfare services, Lunsford and the
League proposed a larger role for the states than was envisioned in
the Mondale/Schroeder bills. Their policy preference, which ultimately shaped the form of the House bill and the final legislation,
arose not only from their professional social service perspective but
also from a deep-seated feeling that the League had been slighted
in the Senate hearings. After the Senate hearings, but before the
Senate vote, Lunsford issued a position paper urging the administration to take the lead in developing child abuse and neglect
policy.[42] Lunsford's statement followed hard on the heels of the
Office of Human Development's announcement that HEW had designated $4 million in additional expenditures for new child abuse
programs and research. The League's statement, which pointedly
omitted reference to the upcoming vote on Mondale's bill, seemed
to ally one of the country's largest and best-known child welfare
organizations with the administration against the passage of categorical child abuse legislation.

Actually, the League's position was somewhat more complex. The
League thought that the Senate bill had been captured by physicians, something that would not have happened if the League had

been better consulted. But Ellen Hoffman of Mondale's staff interpreted Lunsford's actions differently. Lunsford, Hoffman later wrote, "was told that, before he joined the League, the organization had been contacted by the Subcommittee and advised that any contribution—including testimony and legislation recommendations—would be welcome. No response had been received until after the hearings, when Lunsford suddenly appeared and declared the organization's opposition to S.1191."[43]

The consequences of the sharp and public differences between the Senate bill and the League's position gave the administration momentary hope that the legislation could be killed. But after the Senate vote, the White House abandoned efforts to defeat the legislation. HEW officials and the League alike knew that legislation was virtually inevitable and set out to influence its final shape as best they could.

Stanley Thomas, Assistant Secretary for Human Development, was instrumental in convincing the administration and Congress that a mutually acceptable bill could be drafted. He arrived at the House hearings bearing gifts—for instance, a program linking child abuse and drug abuse which interested Representative Peyser—and a general willingness to please without prostrating himself. He toed the party line in his testimony, dutifully reiterating that from fiscal year 1971 through fiscal year 1974 an estimated $242 million would be spent on "protective services which include the immediate intervention and support necessary to prevent continued abuse or neglect . . . ," a comment which caused Brademas to "urge a little more humility" on Thomas.[44] Behind the scenes, however, Thomas was even more important. He mediated the policy disputes and personal dislikes which arose between the Select Education Subcommittee and the Secretary's Office. In the end, the bill Brademas brought to the floor was much more acceptable to the administration than the Mondale/Schroeder bills. The House version altered the Senate version on five important counts:

> 1. Addition of a definition of "child abuse and neglect," terms that were not defined in the Senate bill.
> 2. Creation of a program of funding, not less than 5 percent of the annual appropriation, for grants to states. This was to be separated from the demonstration program, for which public and private entities, including government agencies, organizations, and educational institutions, were eligible.

3. A requirement that in order to receive funds under the state program, states must meet ten criteria. These included having in effect procedures for reporting and investigating reports of child abuse, and having personnel and facilities available for treatment. The state funding program and criteria for it were developed primarily in response to the concerns of the Child Welfare League as discussed earlier.

4. A requirement that child abuse and neglect-related programs funded under the Social Security Act also meet the requirements of the state program.

5. Higher authorizations, $15 million for fiscal 1974, $20 million for fiscal 1975, and $25 million for 1976. The duration of the bill was three years, rather than the five years approved by the Senate.[45]

On December 3, in the pre-Christmas legislative rush, Brademas brought the bill to the floor. He carried a letter from Caspar Weinberger, Secretary of HEW, parts of which he read into the record. The letter stated that the Secretary "does not oppose the measure in its present form."[46] The vote (354 to 36) reflected the administration's hands-off policy and the issue's valence character. Only twenty-four Republicans and twelve Southern Democrats voted nay. To save time, Brademas's and Mondale's staff members reconciled the House and Senate versions. The slightly altered House bill passed the Senate by voice vote on December 20, and the House, again by voice vote, on December 21. The next day Congress went home for the holidays.

The bill that Congress left for the president to sign was a textbook example of compromise in the legislative process. It authorized $85 million to be spent during the next four years. Expenditures were earmarked in three ways: at least 50% of appropriated funds was to be spent on "demonstration" programs (a Mondale preference); at least 5% but no more than 20% was to be awarded as grants to the states (a House preference, and an approach urged by the Child Welfare League), and no more than $1 million was to be spent on the in-house advisory board (the administration did not want public members on an expert, extramural advisory board which was sure to criticize the administration in the manner of all nongovernmental experts). The administration also got its way in nonfiscal matters by convincing Congress not to designate in the bill where in HEW the program was to be housed, instead arranging for its placement in the Office of Child Development (now the Administration on Children, Youth, and Families) by a letter of agreement. The final bill also established a National Center on Child Abuse and Neglect within HEW, defined child abuse, and established requirements for state reporting laws, requirements which had to be met for states to be eligible for state service grants. Eligibility for demonstration grants was not tied to reporting laws.[47]

But textbook-like or not, when Congress returned, President Nixon had still not signed the child abuse bill. For a few days there was some fear that he would allow the bill to become law without his signature. But as one observer noted, "No president fails to take credit when credit is possible." So on January 31, 1974, the Child Abuse Prevention and Treatment Act became Public Law 93-247.

Recurring Maintenance: The Reauthorizations of 1978 and 1981

The bureaucratic engine which was to drive the programs established in CAPTA took much longer to stoke than anyone could have imagined. The National Center for Child Abuse and Neglect (NCCAN), created by the law to coordinate and disseminate program material, remained leaderless for months as political infighting over the eventually successful candidate (Douglas Besharov) and the designation of the position (civil service rather than political) dragged on.

And as NCCAN lumbered, Congress slept. Virtually nothing related to child abuse happened in Congress for the four years of CAPTA's life. There were the standard articles, letters, and pious declarations read into the record, but constituent groups were being addressed, not Congress. Quite simply, child abuse had moved from the discretionary agenda where new issues emerge to the "sporadically recurring agenda" where legislation is periodically considered for reauthorization.[48]

According to schedule, CAPTA was considered for reauthorization in 1977 and given a new lease and a somewhat changed mandate in 1978 in the form of the Child Abuse Prevention and Treatment and Adoption Reform Act (CAPTARA). The reauthorization was completely routine, with the most interesting changes centering on the two issues associated with CAPTA's renewal: child pornography and adoption law reform.

The House version of the CAPTA extension bill (H.R. 6693) proposed penalties of up to twenty years' imprisonment or a $50,000 fine for those convicted of making child pornography and conveying it across state lines. Child pornography was a newly visible issue in 1977, promoted by Dr. Judiann Densen-Gerber and consumed by the insatiable media. Privately, many members of the Select Education Subcommittee felt that the problem, though horrific, had been blown completely out of proportion and that Congress was forced to give it more attention than it warranted. No one interviewed felt the reenactment of CAPTA in any way depended on the infusion of interest generated by child pornography. In fact, just the opposite was true. Committee members and others felt that the child pornography provisions of the House bill took the legislation dangerously close to the intractable problems of obscenity legislation, problems better handled by the Judiciary Committee. The child pornography titles were eventually dropped from the final version of the legislation. Child pornography was regulated in the Sexual Exploitation Act of 1978, which amended Title 18 of the Federal Code (the "Mann Act").

The Senate's new contribution to the child abuse legislation consisted of a section urging more attention to the problems of children in need of adoption. The original Senate bill included a provision for subsidizing the adoption of certain hard-to-place youngsters. This provision was dropped when Senator Alan Cranston (D., Cal.), the bill's sponsor, proposed separate legislation on the problem. Cranston's support for subsidized adoptions was a radical departure from the conventional approach on how to respond to hard-to-place children and it did not win congressional approval in 1978, although it had the backing of the Carter administration.[49] Instead, the Child Abuse Prevention and Treatment and Adoption Reform Act (CAPTARA), signed on April 24, 1978, included a number of more innocuous provisions such as the coordination of federal adoption efforts in HEW and a study of black market adoptions. It also extended a slightly altered version of CAPTA for four years, set spending authorizations comparable to the first legislation, and, importantly, increased the percentage of money designated for state programs from the 1974 requirement of no less than 5% and no more than 20% to a minimum of 25% in fiscal years 1978 and 1979, and 30% in fiscal years 1980 and 1981. This last change was the product of a concerted effort by a large number of individuals and groups dissatisfied with the management of NCCAN. Another safeguard against what was thought to be unresponsive Washington control came with the addition of three public members to the formerly in-house and largely inactive Advisory Board on Child Abuse and Neglect.

The first extension of the child abuse legislation was completely ordinary and uneventful. The changes in the child abuse titles represented the compromises made between squabbling professionals who had moderately differing views of the problem but a joint commitment to retaining the legislation and its service and research monies. The addition of the adoption sections exemplified how a new issue with untested legitimacy could be tied to an issue already established on the legislative agenda. Once it had been reauthorized, congressional supporters of child protection legislation were prepared to go to sleep again, waiting for the law's alarm clock to tell them that it was time to reconsider the legislation.

When the alarm rang in 1981, the child abuse legislation woke up like Rip Van Winkle to an enormously altered legislative world. In the interim, Ronald Reagan had been elected president and the Republicans had gained control of the Senate for the first time in twenty-six years. That year, CAPTARA was almost allowed to expire, its functions to be divided between social service block grants and the newly proposed centralized research efforts of the Department of Health and Human Services (HHS). Only a greatly stripped-down version of CAPTARA survived the first year of the Reagan budget cuts.

CAPTARA was saved at the last minute, reauthorized in the Omnibus Budget Reconciliation Act of 1981. Its rescue, however, had little to do with the merits of the legislation. Rather, it was reprieved as part of a deal with several Southern representatives unhappy with a particular energy proposal in which gas-rich Southern states would have had to increase their use of Northern-produced coal. Liberals required a concession on the child abuse legislation as the price of satisfying the Southerners. Before this trade, the prospects for retaining the child abuse legislation were grim. Senator Jeremiah Denton, who chaired the Subcommittee on Aging, Family, and Human Services, was opposed to most categorical social legislation. In the spring of 1981, he scheduled hearings on the reauthorization of CAPTARA and then abruptly canceled them. Smart money gave the bill little chance of being extended.

A number of people and groups swam against the tide, trying to salvage the program. Senator Cranston, aided by Republican Senators Stafford of Vermont and Weicker of Connecticut, labored to keep CAPTARA from being entirely eliminated or its programs farmed out to social service block grants. They managed to "save" $7 million from the proposed social service block grant (in the Senate's reconciliation bill) to be spent specifically, and separately, on child abuse. Had that bill succeeded, their efforts would nonetheless have been in vain, because Senator Denton had announced that he would amend the Senate's bill on the floor to include the child abuse money in the block grants.

The Child Abuse Coalition, a newly created lobby sponsored by the National Committee for Prevention of Child Abuse, tried to encourage administrative support for reauthorizing CAPTARA. On June 15, Donna Stone, daughter of millionaire Clement Stone (a large Republican party contributor) and the founder of the National Committee, and a number of supporters of the legislation met with Richard Schweiker, Secretary of Health and Human Services. As they walked along the corridor into the Secretary's office more than one visitor noted the many empty offices formerly housing HHS's phalanx of assistant secretaries. (It took seven months for all the assistant secretaries in HHS to be appointed and confirmed, a clear attempt by the Reagan administration to make it difficult for the bureaucracy to be "captured" by the constituents affected by proposed social program cuts.)

The meeting was polite. Present were Schweiker and his daughter Lonnie, who worked in NCCAN during the summer; Dorkus Hardy, the Assistant Secretary for Human Development Services; Anne Cohn and Donna Stone of the National Committee; Tom Birch of the Coalition; Dr. Eli Newberger of Children's Hospital in Boston; and Dr. Frederick Green of Children's Hospital in Washington, D.C. (Green, of course, had resigned in 1973 as Associate Director of the Children's Bureau rather than support the Nixon administration's stand against Mondale's original bill). Though he appeared to have been poorly briefed, the Secretary did express a commitment to federal efforts to prevent and treat child abuse, particularly in maintaining a clearinghouse function to disseminate information. No more specific commitment was forthcoming. The group left feeling the chill of polite but unenthusiastic interest, yet glad they had been able to present their views at all.

From an agenda-setting perspective, this meeting, which seemed at the time to be the last hurrah for a small social program, displayed a certain remarkable symmetry with Mondale's Senate hearings. The federal government acknowledged private charity and physicians as the advocates of the child abuse cause. Official representatives of pesky public welfare organizations were ignored.

Secretary Schweiker reiterated the administration's position that child abuse was a problem best addressed at the state level, sentiments shared by congressional conservatives. This argument was heard again and again throughout the spring and summer of 1981. Though couched in the language of workaday fiscal federalism, the argument also was premised on important and deeply held philosophical tenets. Those opposed to reauthorizing CAPTARA felt that it was morally misguided, and would weaken the disciplinary powers of families through an invasion of family autonomy. JoAnn Gaspar, whom Reagan appointed Deputy Assistant Secretary for Social

Services Policy in HHS, captured conservative mistrust of this type of legislation when she wrote: "I know what yelling is—that is when I raise my voice. But what is 'excessive yelling'? Who determines 'excessive'? My son would probably say that if I yell at him once, that is excessive. So now, we understand domestic violence as any form of mistreatment and neglect as defined by government bureaucrats and professional 'family service' personnel."[50] Social conservatives consciously narrowed the definition of child abuse. Neglect and community culpability vanished. Child abuse became merely the assault of a minor, with all the legal overtones this definition implied.

It is a wonder then that any federal presence was retained, and almost none would have survived if it were not for the exigencies of old-fashioned political horse-trading. When President Reagan signed the Omnibus Reconciliation Act on August 13, 1981, a much weakened version of CAPTARA received a two-year reprieve. The new legislation authorized $19 million for both fiscal year 1982 and fiscal year 1983. Congress earmarked $7 million for grants to the states, retained not more than $2 million for adoption programs, and authorized $10 million to be spent at the discretion of the Secretary on "activities of national significance related to child abuse prevention and treatment."[51] Immediately after the passage of the Reconciliation Act, knowledgeable people in HHS were skeptical that the discretionary money would ever be spent. At that time, most felt that the child abuse legislation would not survive autonomously when the budget knife was applied again.[52]

The future of national child abuse legislation was brighter in the summer of 1983 than it had been in 1981. In both houses of Congress, bills were reported reauthorizing the law at spending levels above those set in 1981. The clear link between rising unemployment and increasing child abuse did much to convince members of Congress of the importance of retaining the law. The future of the legislation may be greatly influenced by the newly proposed "Baby Doe" provisions, however. Here the federal government would provide guidance to states and communities concerning what to do if medical attention or nutrition is withheld from gravely ill newborn infants. This provision rather acrimoniously revives the debate over how to define abuse and neglect.

Interpreting Congressional Agenda Setting

What made it so easy for Mondale to place child abuse on the congressional agenda in 1973, and so difficult for issue partisans to keep it there a mere eight years later with its fortune improving again in just two years? Or, more generally, what does a decade of congressional action on child abuse tell us about agenda setting for social policy in the national legislature? To answer these questions we need to consider in a larger context the rise, fall, and renewed commitment of Congress to alleviate child abuse. We need to analyze the variety of factors which explain congressional agenda setting for social policy: the importance of leadership, the structural opportunities to exercise leadership, a twenty-year liberal plurality in the Senate, and expansive budget procedures.

The study of leadership has fallen out of fashion in political science, a casualty of the empirical revolution and the elusive nature of the topic. But it is through examining leadership that we draw the first general lessons about agenda setting from child abuse. Mondale provided the leadership, vision, and endurance necessary to make child abuse an issue of public policy. Though described by one disgruntled observer as "a minor senator from a minor state who used a minor issue to catapult himself to the vice-presidency," that was not the general evaluation of his efforts against abuse. Rather, Mondale was more often remembered as "truly interested in child welfare," and "a trooper." His personal commitment, consistency, and knowledge of the Senate led people to trust him. Admittedly, championing legislation against child abuse was a safe method of increasing name recognition, and Mondale was testing the presidential waters. However, there was nothing nefarious in Mondale's doing good for the country while doing well for himself. Interest group politics in a liberal democracy is frequently conducted in this manner.

Mondale was aided by his control of the new, unencumbered Subcommittee on Children and Youth. In fact, he sought new issues to claim as part of the territory of his subcommittee. But Mondale's support of child welfare issues was not limited to easy and popular legislation. The much more controversial Child and Family Services Act of 1975 was also considered by that body.

The great expansion of subcommittees and staff gave every senator a pulpit, and a "bully pulpit" at that. The reasons for the rapid growth are many and varied. Specialization is a valued attribute in the Senate, and the proliferation of subcommittees promoted specialization. Specialization encourages technically competent legislation, but this managerial consideration pales in comparison with the political uses of subcommittees. Subcommittees give senators independent power bases early in their careers. Senators *wanted* an expanded subcommittee system for its political value.

This structural accommodation to political considerations yielded important but unforeseen consequences. The enlarged subcommittee system and other institutional reforms designed to democratize Congress probably also contributed to the dilution of party discipline. (Partisanship was also declining among the electorate.) But more important, the proliferation of subcommittees contributed to the increasing size of government.

More committees produced more legislation, which encouraged larger expenditures, which contributed to the appearance of an active (or, alternatively, intrusive) federal government and an "unmanageable" federal budget. Certainly the growth in federal expenditures cannot be completely blamed on the expansion of subcommittees or even on categorical social legislation. But subcommittees provided one vehicle, one aspect of the organizational infrastructure, which permitted active government when the party of active government controlled both houses and the country still had faith in governmental initiatives.

Almost at the same moment that child abuse legislation passed, Congress changed its budget procedures in ways which would ultimately limit the power of authorizing committees to do just what they did in passing CAPTA. The 1974 Congressional Budget and Impoundment Control Act, popularly known as the Budget Reform Act, established a procedure called "reconciliation" through which each chamber could direct its authorizing committees to report legislation "that will cause budget authority, outlays and revenues (as estimated by the CBO) to meet certain targets."[53] It took several years for the Budget Committees to establish themselves, but by 1980 the process was well worked out, and in 1981 President Reagan used it effectively to reshape the federal budget and national spending priorities. Under the Budget Reform Act, congressional lawmaking has been "fiscalized," to use Allen Schick's term: "Legislation now tends to be dominated in dollar terms, and the outcome often turns on whether the measure is perceived to be fiscally responsible and in line with budget policy."[54]

One wonders what effect the fiscalization of lawmaking will have on legislation aimed at social equity. The democratization of Congress, which dates from the early 1960s, coincided with a great cultural ferment in the name of increased social equity. This swing toward equity in what is often called the equity/efficiency cycle began with the civil rights movement. The issue of child abuse played an important, though mostly symbolic, role in the expression of the quest for equity within Congress.

Child abuse legislation proved to be an agenda leader for two other sets of issues: those relating to child care and those relating to personal violence. Child abuse infused child welfare workers with new moral vigor, and provided intellectual and political connections to long-standing issues such as adoption reform and foster care. But perhaps more interestingly, the child abuse legislation gave legitimacy and currency to the consideration of the allied issues of violence, autonomy, and physical safety, including the sexual abuse of children, child pornography, abuse of the elderly, domestic violence, and rape. Of course, each of these "violent deviance" issues had its own partisans and its own separate, special history.[55] But each also benefited from the successful "public use of private deviance" implied by child abuse legislation.

Between 1973 and 1981 Congress considered numerous bills which sought to identify and respond to familial violence, sexual exploitation, or sexual assault. The successful legislation included the creation of the National Center for the Prevention and Control of Rape in NIMH, the Rape Victim Privacy Act, and the Sexual Exploitation Act. Most notable among the legislative failures was the two-time defeat of domestic violence legislation.

The child abuse, rape, and domestic violence legislation all implicitly or explicitly addressed power in the family and power in society, questioning the second-class citizenship of women and, to a lesser degree, children. In the early federal child abuse legislation, and even in the rape legislation—where it must be remembered that one piece of legislation concerned courtroom procedures and a second created a very minor, inexpensive program in NIMH— the challenges to conventional power arrangements were largely sidestepped in the legislative process. For the domestic violence issue, and now for child abuse and rape, conservatives have attempted to transfer emphasis from government's proper intervention against violence to government's improper intervention into the privacy, autonomy, and authority of "the home." For conservatives, the sheltered, private nature of the family supercedes the public protection concerns which underpinned earlier governmental actions.

Of all these issues, child abuse was the most insulated from attack based on the threat to conventional power arrangements. Conservatives as well as liberals acknowledge some fiduciary role for the state in the upbringing of children. But criticisms about governmental intervention were made, sometimes without close attention to the facts. Richard B. Dingman, executive director of the House Republican Study Committee, recently lectured that "the National

Child Abuse Bill [CAPTARA] allows the federal government to take children away from their families,"[56] a statement which is untrue in any but the most trivial sense: CAPTARA funds projects where decisions might occasionally be made to remove children from imminent danger, but only by invoking the proper state laws and procedures. Dingman's implication, that the legislation gave the federal government a warrant to "steal" children from their homes, is patently false. In fact, conservatives usually neglect to mention that only under state laws can children be removed from their homes.

Opponents of the legislation could have more accurately noted that legislation designed as a research and demonstration approach to solving problems of severe physical abuse had been transformed into a commitment to respond to neglect and abuse in its many forms. Indeed, both state administrators and grantees of the CAPTARA legislation derived some satisfaction in noting that child abuse monies from CAPTARA and Title XX were spent on a wide range of children's services. They were quick to note, however, that responding properly to abuse and neglect *required* the provision of a wide range of services.

The national child abuse legislation was good for its sponsors, good for the professionals who supported it, and—though more difficult to prove—probably good for the children whose lives it touched. But the law was pulled into responding to a whole host of complex social problems beyond the scope of its categorical mandate. In this way, the federal child abuse legislation performed like most categorical legislation. It was constructed on the faith of good intentions and the hope that the whole of all categorical social programs will be greater than the sum of their parts. This is rarely so.

7. The Public Use of Private Deviance

In this last chapter we shall review how child abuse achieved the four agendas under study. This review has two purposes beyond presenting a summary of the findings. First, we want to draw the more general lesson of each case. Second, we want to examine if and how the initial construction of the problem on each agenda contributes to the movement toward reprivatizing abuse. Governmental response to abuse and neglect is in a state of flux, and a small but strong minority of social conservatives would like to see governmental responsibility minimized or eliminated. Thus the study will conclude with a discussion of the limits of liberal reform, the limits of defining a problem as private deviance when its causes are also intimately connected with social injustice.

Setting the Public Agenda

Agenda setting is the course by which issues are adopted for governmental consideration and perhaps remedy. Although agenda setting can be approached from an economic or issue-oriented perspective, the focus of this work is on decision making in organizations. The objective was to find out how officials learn about new problems, decide to give them their personal attention, and mobilize their organizations to respond to them. To answer these questions we examined four situations where child abuse achieved important agendas: the U.S. Children's Bureau, the mass and professional media, state legislatures, and Congress. In the process we discovered how child abuse, originally a private-sector charity concern, became additionally a public-sector social welfare issue.

The social problem we call abuse is about a century old, even though evidence of maltreatment exists all through human records. This apparent paradox is resolved by understanding that a social problem is a social construct. A social problem depends not only on the existence of conditions unacceptable to some people, but also on organization to redress those conditions and a modicum of social support for such efforts. The invention of child abuse as a social problem rested in part on the increasingly popular ideal of a "protected" childhood in the home, an ideal which took hold in American culture in the decades after the Civil War. In 1874, New York City was rocked by the reports that Mary Ellen Wilson was regularly beaten by her stepmother. Outraged charity workers and their supporters formed the New York Society for the Prevention of Cruelty to Children. Interest in the problem declined as Progressivism superseded the Scientific Charity movement. It was not until the 1950s and 1960s, when new research was undertaken, that the problem again came to the fore.

By examining how child abuse achieved these agendas we expected to understand better how new categorical social service policies are initiated. It was immediately evident, however, that child abuse was emblematic of another group of policy issues dealing with violence in intimate situations. Governmental response to child abuse made it easier for issue partisans to promote more sensitive governmental response to rape, as well as recognition of such "new" problems as spouse abuse, child sexual abuse, child pornography, and abuse of the elderly. In this sense, child abuse was an agenda-leading issue.

The valence, i.e., noncontroversial, character of child abuse allowed its rapid adoption on each agenda. Initially the problem was constructed as parenting gone crazy, the awful violence that individual adults inflicted on individual children. This construction gave the issue support from conservatives as well as liberals. Indeed, when abuse first achieved governmental agendas, all but the most orthodox conservatives felt that the government's fiduciary role toward children included protecting them from physical violence. Policymakers were very wary, though, of associating abuse with physical discipline. They did not want to appear to be undermining the "natural authority" of parents over their children and were careful not to construct the problem as one of unequal power within the family. Such a construction (redressing unequal power within the family) defeated the second Domestic Violence bill in Congress.

Contemporary governmental interest in abuse and neglect was part of a larger social current pushing issues of equity to the fore. In the period when abuse was rediscovered, the civil rights, welfare rights, and feminist movements captured the imagination of many people. Although the underlying problems raised by these movements—racism, poverty, and patriarchy—were not adequately addressed by minority scholarships, school lunches, or "equal pay for equal work" legislation, a spirit of optimism and good will prevailed. In part this generous spirit was a result of the greatest economic boom in American history—real GNP more than doubled between 1950 and 1970. Consequently, governmental support of child protection did not invoke a zero-sum argument.[1] Funding for child abuse programs, never large in any event, was only marginally in competition with the war in Vietnam, Food Stamps, or subsidized airport construction.

Over a period of twenty years, child abuse was *recognized, adopted, priorities* about its importance set, and interest *maintained* in three public institutions and the mass and professional media. First, the U.S. Children's Bureau became interested in child protective services and then physical abuse. Its model child abuse reporting law (aided by escalating media coverage) spurred states to adopt similar legislation. The demands of influential lobbyists for child protective services, good service models, and adequate funds prompted Congress to pass legislation providing research and demonstration support and, to a lesser degree, social service monies. The history of agenda setting for this issue shows clearly how one public institution helps to set the agendas of others.

The Children's Bureau

The Children's Bureau provides a perfect example of "unplanned" agenda-setting. The Bureau was, first and foremost, an "issue-sensing" organization. After identifying an emerging child welfare or health problem, the Bureau's staff, aided by outside experts, undertook research to develop practical responses. In 1955, the Bureau learned of the American Humane Association's research on child protective services and immediately included the findings in its communication stream. The priority of the problem increased when the Bureau also became interested in the research by Dr. C. Henry Kempe on the battered-child syndrome. To encourage reporting, the Children's Bureau drafted (in 1962) and circulated (in 1963) a model child abuse reporting law.

The Bureau committed funds out of its small yearly research budget to pay for the development of the model statute. Immediately thereafter, however, the Bureau's research budget grew astronomically. Congress bankrolled a new era of research by the Children's Bureau when it passed the 1960 Maternal and Child Welfare amendments to the Social Security Act. (The money was not available until fiscal year 1962.) The issue of child abuse benefited from being in the right place at the right time. Projects on child abuse received a large share of the newly available research funds. Between 1962 and 1968, the Bureau spent an estimated one million dollars on child abuse and family law research.

These funds changed the nature of the Children's Bureau, however. Very rapidly, the Bureau went from being a issue-sensing and internal research agency to a grant-managing agency. Consequently, when the Nixon administration wanted to reorganize HEW on a functional rather than population basis, it practically destroyed the Bureau by assigning the Maternal and Child Health programs, which funded most of the Bureau's research, to the Health Services and Mental Health Administration. The agency had no more money for outside research and went into rapid decline.

Only the national child abuse legislation, which created the National Center for Child Abuse and Neglect (NCCAN) and placed it within the Bureau, saved the Bureau from total obscurity. But the remission was short. President Reagan's budget cuts pared research on abuse and neglect from $17 million in fiscal year 1980 to $2 million in fiscal year 1982.[2] In October, 1981, the Administration on Children, Youth, and Families, where the Bureau now resides, began the layoffs and job changes which were designed to eliminate 443 jobs by fiscal year 1983, including thirty-three Washington positions in the Bureau and twenty-five in the regions. Such budget and staffing cuts signal an extremely limited presence for the Bureau and NCCAN in the early Reagan administration. Even the increased appropriations expected in the 1983 Reconciliation Act cannot easily replace the expertise lost through staffing cuts.

Media Attention to Abuse

The role of the media was not important when child abuse first achieved the agenda of the Children's Bureau. But initial consideration in state legislatures and Congress benefited from sustained coverage in professional journals, popular magazines, and newspapers. Between 1950 and 1980, professional journals carried 1,756 articles on abuse and neglect, popular magazines published another 124 articles, and the *New York Times* printed 652 stories on the subject. Virtually all of them were published after Dr. C. Henry Kempe's famous article "The Battered-Child Syndrome" appeared in the July 7, 1962 edition of the *Journal of the American Medical Association*. Indeed, Kempe's article so focused attention on the problem of child abuse that it is customarily used to date the "rediscovery" of the issue in this century.

This ever-growing interest in child abuse is somewhat inconsistent with the issue-attention cycle proposed by Anthony Downs.

His formulation suggests that the public wearies of domestic problems when the essential conflicts of value—especially the need for redistribution—become evident. The cycle has five stages: "the problem stage, alarmed discovery and euphoric enthusiasm, realizing the cost of significant progress, gradual decline of intense public interest and the post problem stage."[3] Downs repeatedly refers to media response as one of the engines that drives the cycle, although he does not define the issue-attention cycle solely in terms of media coverage. But Downs does not detail the media's own attention cycle, either its duration or the causes of sustained media interest. Examining media coverage of child abuse offered a useful opportunity to investigate these questions.

The link between the professional and mass media proved extraordinarily important in initiating and sustaining mass media—and thus popular—interest in child abuse. The message of "The Battered-Child Syndrome" was repeated in *Time* and the *Saturday Evening Post* within weeks of its publication. The magazines learned of Kempe's research through an AMA press release. Over the years, the institutional links between professional and mass media—press releases and science and medicine beat reporting—kept new professional information flowing to popular magazines and newspapers. Research supported by the Children's Bureau (and later NCCAN and other public and private sources) created endless numbers of "events" for the media to cover. The variety and volume of research was a product of the natural course of the research cycle, where a problem is simultaneously narrowed and broadened. This narrowing, called topic differentiation, meant that some scholars were concentrating on very specific aspects of the abuse, like the association of illegitimacy and maltreatment. The broadening, called issue aggregation, meant that other scholars were connecting abuse with analogous concerns, like domestic violence.

Somewhat surprisingly, research reports constitute the major source of the *increase* in newspaper coverage (at least in the *New York Times*). In the *Times* and elsewhere, these reports are often found in the soft-news sections of the paper. The articles offered readers the titillation of violence and the palliatives of medicine and social work. The appeal of "science" gave abuse and neglect the legitimacy necessary for coverage in respectable papers.[4]

Would media attention decline if research funds continued to decline? I imagine so, but not quite for the reasons Downs proposed. Coverage may decline because there is less to report. There may be less to report because there is less research money spent. And there is less research money because of the conflicting values over the size of the budget and the role of the federal government in social programs. Conflicting values over the propriety of intervening in the family are not directly driving the budgetary decision making about federal child abuse legislation, although the social conservatives like the Moral Majority have raised these questions. In ways not evident during an era of plenty and growth, the issue-attention cycle may be significantly affected by larger macroeconomic and political concerns.

The downward spiral of decreasing research and media coverage may induce further programmatic and policy changes as well. The consequences of reduced research and coverage could include less public awareness and declining "demand" for public programs. In the long run, reporting of suspected cases to welfare offices might decline as well, the product of citizen apathy and fiscal difficulties in staffing reporting and service systems. A public convinced of bureaucratic unresponsiveness would be further discouraged to report. The great fear of advocates of public policy against abuse is that declining media coverage and declining reporting will be used to assert that the actual incidence of abuse is declining.

In point of fact, child abuse and neglect are probably increasing, thus the number of new cases reported has remained constant or even increased in many areas. Of course, it is virtually impossible to determine how many cases of abuse or neglect occur in any time period. Disagreements over definitions and standards of evidence, and difficulties in reporting and enumeration, prevent an accurate count in any year, let alone an accurate, proper comparison across years. Nonetheless, we do know a great deal about the social conditions associated with abuse and neglect. These problems, though found everywhere, are more prevalent in families with limited economic resources, current unemployment, or high stress.[5] When family income declines and unemployment worsens, the actual and reported incidence of abuse and neglect may increase for a while. This has been the recent experience in New York City, where "the number of reports has risen from 14,300 in 1976 to more than 19,300 last year [1980], when 32,078 children were involved. More than half the reports prove unfounded, and part of the increase is credited to greater public awareness. But social agency officials believe that because of unemployment, poor housing and other situations that cause stress, there has been an actual increase in violence in society in general and in violence directed against children."[6] The increases in the budget proposed in 1983 for the federal child abuse law were a direct result of efforts to keep Congress informed about the link between recession and abuse.

131

State Legislatures

Initial state response to child abuse took the form of reporting laws. The laws themselves cost the states almost nothing and thus, at minimum, abuse is likely to remain formally on the agenda. The laws, however, "invoke" other expensive public systems, ranging from child welfare services to the juvenile court, and these systems are currently hard-pressed to meet the demands engendered by large-scale reporting.

The low cost of reporting laws, both monetarily and in terms of political capital, accounted for their rapid initial adoption. Beginning in 1963, state legislatures were bombarded with model statutes on reporting child abuse. The first was promulgated by the Children's Bureau, but the American Humane Association, the Council of State Governments, the American Medical Association, and the American Academy of Pediatrics soon offered competing models.

Taking these models as cues, every state passed a child abuse reporting law between 1963 and 1967, a diffusion of innovation five times more rapid than average.[7] This extraordinarily rapid adoption can be explained by two factors. First, reporting laws allowed state legislators to display no-cost public rectitude. (Only Illinois passed an appropriation with its first reporting law.) No monetary cost, combined with the opportunity to be on the "side of the angels" by protecting children, made these laws extremely attractive to legislators. Child abuse reporting laws were perfect valence issues. Their noncontroversial character brings us to the second factor promoting rapid diffusion: a narrow definition of the problem and a simple solution. In the initial round of lawmaking, the problem was seen as the necessity to encourage the reporting of physical abuse by physicians who were generally reluctant to become involved in any health problems having legal consequences. Children's safety could be served by requiring physicians to report and by protecting physicians from liability for reporting in good faith.

In most states, reporting laws have changed substantially. From a policy perspective, the most important change is the addition of protective custody provisions, allowing a state to remove a child from his or her home (usually for three working days) when harm seems imminent. During that time, the state must petition the court for "temporary" custody if the situation warrants it. In common parlance, the child then becomes "a ward of the court," but permanent parental rights are not severed. The advent of protective custody provisions gave child welfare workers (and others) a much stronger tool for intervention in families, although the clauses themselves authorize only short-term separations. These provisions reshaped the legislation, changing it from a public health focus to a child welfare focus. Unfortunately, no figures exist on how frequently protective custody clauses have been invoked nationwide. But we do know that "each year approximately 150,000 'child neglect' proceedings are heard by juvenile courts throughout the country."[8]

Both protective and temporary custody practices have increasingly been criticized from three quarters. Noninterventionist jurists argue that lenient custody standards allow children to be removed from their homes for poverty-related reasons, which in practice means that minority children are more at risk of being separated from their caretakers.[9] Arguing from different premises, a group of prominent psychoanalysts asserts that intervention ought to be limited to the most extreme cases of abuse or neglect because the interruption of psychological parenthood, especially the interruption of a child's belief that "parents are omniscient and all-powerful," disrupts proper child development.[10] Conservative social critics, often fundamentalist in their religious beliefs, join the psychoanalysts in opposing intervention in the family because they too support traditional, often patriarchal, lines of authority in the family.

It is clear that faith in governmental intervention, so prominent in the early 1970s, has been tempered.[11] A slow economy makes financing intervention more problematic, and the dearth of good, short-term (and long-term) placements makes intervention less clearly beneficial for a child. This movement toward more limited intervention can be seen in the IJA-ABA *Standards Relating to Abuse and Neglect* published in 1981, which suggests that "coercive state intervention should be premised upon specific harms that a child has suffered or is likely to suffer."[12] (The draft standards promulgated by IJA-ABA were even more anti-interventionist and failed to pass the American Bar Association's House of Delegates for that reason.[13]) A policy of limited intervention also conforms to public opinion on the proper response to child neglect. In a recent study, Norman Polansky and his associates found a strong preference for traditional social-casework help for neglectful families, judging this response kinder and more adequate (they use the term "sufficient") than temporary or permanent familial breakup.[14]

No doubt a strong intervention law and a weak response system are programatically and politically unbalanced. Thus a hearty respect for cultural differences and the humility to recognize the limits of intervention are to be applauded. But these changes correct what is wrong with the *law*. The challenge is to make the "response system"—the market, public action, and community efforts—better.

It will be interesting to see if state legislatures adopt this more limited approach to abuse and neglect. Indeed, the shift in emphasis is so substantial that such an effort might qualify as a new case of agenda setting. It will be especially interesting to see who leads the fight. For issue partisans, and perhaps for the general public, the new construction of the problem does not have the same valence character, and new legislation no longer offers supporters the attraction of no-cost public rectitude.

Congress

Strong personal leadership, and procedures supporting incremental social change, brought child abuse to the congressional agenda. In March, 1973, Senator Mondale introduced legislation providing funds to support research and demonstration programs to combat abuse and neglect. In January, 1974, President Nixon signed a somewhat altered version of the bill which also provided social service funds available to the states. Several years earlier, Representative Mario Biaggi introduced a number of bills to create a nationwide child abuse reporting system. Framed as amendments to the Social Security Act, none of his bills was ever reported out of the Ways and Means Committee.

In part, Mondale succeeded where Biaggi failed because by 1973 child abuse was more firmly established on other agendas. But Mondale also benefited from his well-known commitment to child welfare and his position as the chair of the newly created Subcommittee on Children and Youth. In fact, he was looking for issues on which to establish the subcommittee's reputation, and the Child Abuse Prevention and Treatment Act (CAPTA) was the first piece of legislation promoted from that forum.[15] Mondale also operated under the "old" congressional budget process, which allowed, if not encouraged, incremental social change through categorical legislation because spending limits were not imposed on authorizing committees.

In 1978, CAPTA was routinely reenacted in a slightly different form as the Child Abuse Prevention and Treatment and Adoption Reform Act (CAPTARA). Maintaining child abuse on the congressional agenda during this first reauthorization was easy. But the situation had altered dramatically when the second reauthorization occurred. By 1981, conservative opposition to governmental "interference" in the family, Republican commitment to a smaller federal presence in social programs, and, most importantly, a fully functioning "new" congressional budget process threatened the existence of CAPTARA. The Omnibus Reconciliation Act of 1981 reauthorized CAPTARA, but only because of political horse-trading and only through fiscal year 1983. The authorized funding level for research and demonstration projects declined from $17 million in fiscal year 1980 to $10 million in fiscal years 1982 and 1983, but the May, 1982 Federal Register showed that the Office of Human Development Services planned to fund only $2 million worth of research.[16] The budget allocations for the proposed House bill (H.R. 1904) raise spending for CAPTARA from $30.8 million in fiscal year 1984 to $34.7 million in fiscal year 1987.

The reauthorization of CAPTARA through the 1981 Omnibus Reconciliation Act shows the importance of budget procedures in congressional agenda setting. The "old" budget system, without centrally imposed limits on outlays, encouraged what public-choice theorists fear most in legislative bodies—logrolling without cost-benefit constraints. The explosion of subcommittees, which gave senators (and representatives) institutional power bases early in their careers, complemented the "old" budget system. And a post-war economic boom of unprecedented magnitude made congressional policy initiatives even more appealing.

Budget considerations did not figure at all in the passage of CAPTA in 1974. In over fifty hours of interviews with the people most active in passing this bill, only Stanley Thomas, the former Assistant Secretary for Human Development, mentioned the budget process. But in 1981 and again in 1983, the budget was the major consideration among policy makers.

Certainly categorical social policy initiatives like CAPTARA have not caused the federal budget problem. Rather, growth in social expenditure comes primarily from the expansion of income transfer programs. In 1951, the major social programs constituted 22.0% of all federal budget outlays, compared to 48.2% in 1981.[17] But categorical social initiatives do raise other interesting questions about governance. In the absence of cultural support for even minor redistributive efforts, how are the resulting segmented demands for social intervention met? One answer is to encourage interest group politics, where many social problems are constructed as self-contained and essentially noneconomic. The old congressional budget process, aided by Democratic majorities, supported this method of responding to social problems.

The new budget process and hard economic times are clearly changing the process of agenda setting in Congress. Allen Schick has already prophesied stronger party discipline as well as the "fiscalization" of issues, that is, judging the merits of a law by its fiscal impact.[18] New human services legislation whose cost-effectiveness is difficult to demonstrate may fare badly in this policy-making system, even if Democrats control both houses.

But just *how* badly human services legislation will fare is uncertain. The political advantages of promoting specific policies accrue to conservatives and liberals alike. Already we see very conservative legislators promoting new categorical social legislation. Senator Jeremiah Denton, Chair of the Subcommittee on Aging, Family, and Human Services, was willing to let the authorization for CAPTARA lapse during the 1981 reconciliation process. At the same time, however, he was promoting the "Teenage Chastity Act," which originally carried a $30 million price tag.[19] More recently, Denton supported the addition of a new provision to the proposed 1983 reauthorization of CAPTARA which would establish guidelines against withholding medical care and nutrition from profoundly ill newborn babies. The message of his actions is clear: conservatives as well as liberals face the political reality that it is often better to be for something specific than against something vague.

The Limits of Liberal Reform

How did child abuse, the quintessential valence issue, become so controversial? The answer lies in the tensions inherent in incremental social change, i.e., "liberal reform." Governmental action was instigated against a small but severe problem—violent, and thus by definition, deviant, parenting. At a philosophical level the consensus needed to initiate governmental action rested on the belief that such acts ought not to be protected by the private status of the family.

Early in the agenda-setting process, this essentially medical, deviant, individual, and classless construction of abuse masked its social context. The physicians who promoted public interest in abuse, particularly Kempe, were not the perpetrators of a willing deception. They described the problem they saw according to their training as doctors. Their research, which provided so much of the early evidence supporting governmental action, reported instances of extremely brutal physical abuse. From their experience, the belief that abuse was individual and psychopathological in origin was appropriate.

But abuse and neglect do not come in discrete increments separable from family stress and social inequities like poverty, racism, and patriarchy. And once on the agenda, the content of child abuse policy began to reflect these connections. State legislatures, consciously or not, reinforced these essential connections by broadening the statutory definitions of abuse and neglect. When protective custody clauses were added, the reporting laws lost their public health character and clearly became child welfare statutes. At the national level, the research and services funded by CAPTA explicitly sought comprehensive explanations and integrated service models, even though a narrow construction of abuse was consciously used to create the consensus responsible for passing the legislation.

The social and economic antecedents of abuse were acknowledged everywhere except during agenda setting, and therein lies one dilemma of liberal reform. This discrepancy now places child abuse programs in an unfavorable light. Simultaneously, they appear to have exceeded the limited intent of the politicians who created them, while failing to redress the root causes of the problem.

The scenario of having done too much and too little is one consequence of liberal reform. Lacking support for significant social reordering, American reformers are faced with two unsatisfactory alternatives. They can support incremental change, retaining some hope of success but knowing their efforts are not adequate to the problem. Or they can support more comprehensive change whose time may never come. In the liberal state, the "good" usually triumphs over the "best," at least for a while.

Notes

Preface

1. Hugh Heclo, *A Government of Strangers* (Washington, D.C.: The Brookings Institution, 1977), p. xii.

Chapter 1

1. "Child Abuse Prevention Act, S.1191" *Hearings before the Subcommittee on Children and Youth of the Committee on Labor and Public Welfare*, U.S. Senate, Ninety-third Congress, First Session, March 23, 1973, pp. 49–51; hereafter cited as Senate Hearings, March 1973.

2. Senate Hearings, March 1973, p. 52.

3. With the extensions of CAPTA in 1978 and 1981 a total of $160 million was authorized to fight abuse, neglect, and later to promote adoption reform, not all of which was appropriated as budget trimming became more important.

4. The entry "cruelty to children," with its somewhat old-fashioned connotation, appeared intermittently before this time, and early articles on the battered-child syndrome, child abuse, physical abuse of children, etc., were indexed under this heading. The Library of Congress changed its primary index entry to "child abuse" in 1968 and most of the major indexes followed suit.

5. E. E. Schattschneider, *The Semi-Sovereign People* (New York: Holt, Rinehart and Winston, 1960), p. 71.

6. By stating that a culture does not view a particular set of actions as a social problem, I do not mean to imply that the actions are necessarily ethically acceptable, or even that the only standard for ethical judgment is one which is specific to the situation or the time period. What I am arguing for is the realization that cultures *vary* in their recognition and definition of problems.

7. For an elaboration of these points see Malcolm Spector and John I. Kitsuse, "Social Problems: A Re-Formulation," *Social Problems* 21, no. 2 (Fall 1973): 145–159; Armand L. Mauss, "Introduction: Promises and Problems in American Society," in Armand L. Mauss and Julie Camille Wolfe, eds., *This Land of Promises: The Rise and Fall of Social Problems in America* (New York: J. B. Lippincott Co., 1977), pp. 1–23; and Barbara J.

Nelson, "Helpseeking from Public Authorities: Who Arrives at the Agency Door?" *Policy Sciences* 12, no. 1 (August 1980): 175–192.

8. Neil Smelser, *Theory of Collective Behavior* (New York: Free Press, 1962).

9. For a discussion of a similar phenomenon, public response to social movements, see John D. McCarthy and Mayer N. Zald, "Resource Mobilization and Social Movements: A Partial Theory," *American Journal of Sociology* 82, no. 6 (May 1977): 1212–1241. McCarthy and Zald divide the public into constituents, adherents, bystanders, and opponents (p. 1221).

10. Phillipe Ariès, *Centuries of Childhood: A Social History of Family Life*, trans. Robert Baldick, (New York: Vintage Books, 1962); Lawrence Stone, *The Family, Sex and Marriage in England, 1500–1800* (New York: Harper and Row, 1977), pp. 147–81; and Edward Shorter, *The Making of the Modern Family* (New York: Basic Books, 1975), pp. 255–268.

11. Elbridge T. Gerry, "The Relation of Societies for the Prevention of Cruelty to Children to Child-Saving Work," *Proceedings* of the National Conference of Charities and Corrections 1882, pp. 129–130, in Robert H. Bremner, ed., *Children and Youth in America: A Documentary History*, vol. 2, (Cambridge, Mass.: Harvard University Press, 1970), p. 196.

12. See, for example, "The 'New Education' and The Old Ideals" in Bernard Wishy, *The Child and the Republic: The Dawn of Modern American Child Nurture* (Philadelphia: University of Pennsylvania Press, 1968), pp. 136–158; Robert H. Wiebe, *The Search For Order:1877–1920* (New York: Hill and Wang, 1967); Ellen DuBois, *Feminism and Suffrage: The Emergence of an Independent Women's Movement in America, 1848–1869* (Ithaca, New York: Cornell University Press, 1978); and David Montgomery, *Beyond Equality: Labor and Radical Republicans, 1862–1872* (New York: Vintage, 1967).

13. Stanley N. Katz, "Legal History and Family History: The Child, the Family, and the State," address to the Boston College Law School, April 25, 1980, p. 7. See also Philip Greven, *The Protestant Temperament: Patterns of Child-Rearing, Religious Experience and the Self in Early America* (New York: Alfred A. Knopf, 1977).

14. The *New York Times*, April 22, 1874, p. 8.

15. Sydney H. Coleman, *Humane Society Leaders in America* (Albany, N.Y.: the American Humane Association, 1924), pp. 65–89: "Elbridge T. Gerry and the Prevention of Cruelty to Children."

16. The legal details are based on Mason P. Thomas, Jr., "Child Abuse and Neglect Part I: Historical Overview, Legal Matrix, and Social Perspectives," *North Carolina Law Review* 50 (February 1972): 293–349. The details of the case were reassembled through newspaper accounts. See the *New York Times* on the following dates in 1874: April 10 (p. 8), April 11 (p. 2), April 22 (p. 8), June 2 (p. 8), December 7 (pp. 3–4), December 27 (p. 12), and December 29 (p. 2).

17. The *New York Times*, December 29, 1874, p. 2. Two engravings of Ellen Conners can be found in the New York Society for the Prevention

of Cruelty to Children's (unpublished) *Annual Report*, 1876, p. 73. See also Catherine J. Ross, "The Lessons of the Past: Defining and Controlling Child Abuse in the United States," in George Gerbner, Catherine J. Ross, and Edward Zigler, eds., *Child Abuse: An Agenda for Action* (New York: Oxford University Press, 1980), pp. 63–81.

18. Elizabeth Pleck, "Policing the Violent Family: The Humane Societies," unpublished paper given at the Bunting Institute, Radcliffe College, 1980, pp. 3–7.

19. "Proceedings of the Conference on the Care of Dependent Children Held at Washington, D.C.; January 25, 1909," U.S. Senate, Sixtieth Congress, Second Session, Document no. 721, (Washington, D.C.: United States Government Printing Office, 1909), p. 9.

20. William Schultz, *The Humane Movement in the United States, 1910–1922* (New York: Columbia University Press, 1924), pp. 223–228, in Bremner, ed., *Children and Youth* 2, pp. 217–219.

21. C. C. Carstens, "Who Shall Protect the Children?" *Survey* 51 (1923–24): 93.

22. Homer Folks, *Care of Destitute, Dependent, and Delinquent Children* (New York: J. B. Lyon Co., 1902), pp. 173–175, in Bremner, ed., *Children and Youth* 2, p. 213.

23. Josephine Shaw Lowell, "Report on the Institutions for the Care of Destitute Children of the City of New York," reprinted from the *New York State Board of Charities Annual Report for the Year 1885* (Albany, N.Y., 1886), pp. 167–243, in *Care of Dependent Children in the Late Nineteenth and Early Twentieth Centuries* (New York: Arno Press, 1974). The New York SPCC refused to be inspected by the State Board of Charities, and went to court to establish the fact that it was not charity but an arm of the police department. It won. See The People of the State of New York, *ex. rel.* The State Board of Charities *v.* the New York Society of the Prevention of Cruelty to Children, 161 NY, pp. 239–240, 248, in Bremner, ed., *Children and Youth* 2, p. 197, and Coleman, *Humane Society Leaders*, p. 83.

24. John Caffey, "Multiple Fractures in the Long Bones of Infants Suffering from Chronic Subdural Hematoma," *American Journal of Roentgenology* 56 (August 1946): 163–173; F. N. Silverman, "The Roentgen Manifestations of Unrecognized Skeletal Trauma in Infants," *American Journal of Roentgenology, Radium Therapy and Nuclear Medicine* 69 (March 1953): 413–426; John Caffey, "Some Traumatic Lesions in Growing Bones Other Than Fractures and Dislocation—Clinical and Radiological Features," *British Journal of Radiology* 30 (May 1957): 225–238.

25. For a review of the early social work research on physical child abuse, see David G. Gil, *Violence against Children: Physical Child Abuse in the United States* (Cambridge, Mass.: Harvard University Press, 1973), pp. 20–21.

26. C. Henry Kempe et al., "The Battered-Child Syndrome," *The Journal of the American Medical Association* 181, 1 (July 7, 1962): 17–24.

27. Ibid., p. 17.

28. Ibid., p. 24, my emphasis.

29. California Penal Code, Sec. 11161.5, in Jeanne M. Giovannoni and Rosina M. Becerra, *Defining Child Abuse* (New York: The Free Press, 1979), p. 6.

30. PL 93–247, 1974, Sec. 2.

31. See Leroy H. Pelton, "Child Abuse and Neglect: The Myth of Class-lessness," in Leroy H. Pelton, ed., *The Social Context of Child Abuse and Neglect* (New York: Human Sciences Press, 1981), pp. 23–38; and Gil, *Violence against Children*, pp. 133–198.

32. National Conference for Family Violence Researchers, University of New Hampshire, Durham, N.H., July 21, 1981. Professor Gelles is a coauthor with Murray A. Straus and Suzanne K. Steinmetz of *Beyond Closed Doors: Violence in the American Family* (New York: Anchor Books, 1980).

33. For a good summary of the attempts at measuring and estimating child abuse, see Richard J. Gelles, "Violence toward Children in the United States," in Richard Bourne and Eli H. Newberger, eds., *Critical Perspectives on Child Abuse* (Lexington, Mass.: D. C. Heath and Company, 1979), pp. 53–68. The studies cited here are "One Child Dies Daily from Abuse: Parent Probably Was Abuser," *Pediatric News* 9 (April 1975): 3; Gil, *Violence against Children*, pp. 58–60; and Richard Light,"Abused and Neglected Children in America: A Study of Alternative Policies," *Harvard Educational Review* 43 (November 1973): 556–598.

34. Kempe et al., "The Battered-Child Syndrome," pp. 17–24.

35. "The Battered-Child Syndrome" editorial in the *Journal of the American Medical Association* 181, no. 1 (July 7, 1962): 42.

36. Gilbert Y. Steiner, *The Futility of Family Policy* (Washington, D.C.:The Brookings Institution, 1980), pp. 167–170.

37. "The National Study on Child Neglect and Abuse Reporting" (Denver: The Child Protection Division, the American Humane Association, 1981), pp. 6–7.

38. Stephen J. Pfoll, "The 'Discovery' of Child Abuse," *Social Problems* 24, no. 3 (February 1977): 310–323; and Steven Antler, "Child Abuse: An Emerging Social Priority," *Social Work* 23 (January 1978): 58–61.

39. See, for example, Peter Conrad, "The Discovery of Hyperkinesis: Notes on the Medicalization of Deviant Behavior," *Social Problems* 23 (October 1975): 12–21; Russell P. Dobash and R. Emerson Dobash, "Community Response to Violence against Wives: Charivari, Abstract Justice and Patriarchy," *Social Problems* 28 (June 1981): 564–581; Michel Foucault, *Discipline and Punish: The Birth of the Prison* (London: Allen Lane, 1977).

40. David Mechanic, *Medical Sociology* (New York: Free Press, 1978, second edition), p. 44.

41. Edward Sagarin, *Deviants and Deviance: An Introduction to the Study of Disvalued People and Behavior* (New York: Praeger, 1975), pp. 221–225.

42. John A. Denton, *Medical Sociology* (Boston: Houghton Mifflin Co., 1978), pp. 21–22.

43. Zillah Eisenstein, *The Radical Future of Liberal Feminism* (New York: Longman, 1981).

Chapter 2

1. Sections of this chapter derive from my earlier work. See Barbara J. Nelson (with the assistance of Thomas Lindenfeld), "Setting the Public Agenda: The Case of Child Abuse," in Judith V. May and Aaron B. Wildavsky, eds., *The Policy Cycle* (Beverly Hills, Cal.: Sage Publications, 1978), pp. 17–41; Barbara J. Nelson, "The Politics of Child Abuse and Neglect: New Governmental Recognition for an Old Problem," *Child Abuse and Neglect: The International Journal* 3 (Winter 1979): 99–105; and Barbara J. Nelson, "Reviewing Child Abuse Policy in America: A Social Service Approach," *Policy Studies Journal* 9, no. 3 (Winter 1980): 455–463.

2. For an excellent review of the elitism-pluralism debates, see chapter 1, "Recent Theories of Democracy and the Classical Myth," in Carole Pateman, *Participation and Democratic Theory* (Cambridge: Cambridge University Press, 1970), pp. 1–21.

3. Roger W. Cobb and Charles D. Elder, *Participation in American Politics: The Dynamics of Agenda-Building* (Boston: Allyn and Bacon, Inc., 1972), pp. 85, 86.

4. Roger W. Cobb et al., "Agenda Building as a Comparative Process," *American Political Science Review* 70, no. 1 (March 1976): 126–138.

5. Nelson Polsby, *Political Innovation in America: The Politics of Policy Initiation* (New Haven, Conn.: Yale University Press, 1984).

6. Matthew Crenson, *The Un-Politics of Air Pollution* (Baltimore: The Johns Hopkins Press, 1971); Charles O. Jones, *Clean Air* (Pittsburgh: University of Pittsburgh Press, 1975); Edward Wenk, Jr., *The Politics of the Ocean* (Seattle: University of Washington Press, 1972); and Gil Ohmen and Lester Lave, *Clearing the Air: Reform of the Clean Air Act* (Washington, D.C.: The Brookings Institution, 1981).

7. Fay Lomax Cook, "Crime and the Elderly: The Emergence of a Policy Issue," in Dan A. Lewis, ed., *Reactions to Crime* (Beverly Hills, Cal.: Sage, 1981); John Creighton Campbell, "The Old People Boom and Japanese Policy Making," *Journal of Japanese Studies* 5, no. 2 (1972): 321–357, and "Agenda Setting and Small Programs: The Development of Old Age Policy in Japan" (University of Michigan, August 1979), mimeo.

8. Richard A. Rettig, *Cancer Crusade* (Princeton, N.J.: Princeton University Press, 1977), and Theodore R. Marmor, *The Politics of Medicare* (Chicago: Aldine Publishing Co., 1973).

9. Jo Freeman, *The Politics of Women's Liberation* (New York: David McKay Co., 1975); Janet K. Boles, *The Politics of the Equal Rights Amendment: Conflict and the Decision Process* (New York: Longman, 1979); Sara

Evans, *Personal Politics: The Roots of the Feminist Movement in the Civil Rights Movement and New Left* (New York: Alfred A. Knopf, 1979); Drude Dahlerup, "The Socialization of Politics: An Approach to the Study of Non-Decision Making, Which Keeps Women's Issues Out of Political Agenda," joint ECPR/IPSA Conference, Lancaster (England), March 29–April 4, 1981; and Joyce Gelb and Marion Lief Palley, *Women and Public Policies* (Princeton, N.J.: Princeton University Press, 1982).

10. Jack L. Walker, "The Diffusion of Knowledge, Policy Communities and Agenda Setting: The Relationship between Knowledge and Power," in John Tropman, et al., eds. *New Strategic Perspectives on Social Policy* (London: Pergamon Press, 1981), pp. 75–96; Jack L. Walker, "Setting the Agenda in the U.S. Senate: A Theory of Problem Selection," *British Journal of Political Science* 7 (October 1977): 423–445; Jack L. Walker, "The Origins and Maintenance of Interest Groups in America," *American Political Science Review* 77, no. 2 (June 1983): 390–406; Virginia Gray, "Innovation in the States: A Diffusion Study," *American Political Science Review* 67 (December 1973): 1174–1185; Robert Eyestone, "Confusion, Diffusion and Innovation," *American Political Science Review* 71 (June 1977): 441–447; Richard M. Cyert and James G. March, *Behavioral Theory of the Firm* (Englewood Cliffs, N.J.: Prentice-Hall, 1963); Gerald Zaltman et al., *Innovations and Organizations* (New York: Wiley Interscience, 1973); James Q. Wilson, "Innovation in Organization: Notes Toward a Theory," in James D. Thompson, ed., *Approach to Organizational Design* (Pittsburgh: University of Pittsburgh Press, 1966), pp. 194–218; and Terry M. Moe, *The Organization of Interests* (Chicago: University of Chicago Press, 1980).

11. Malcolm Spector and John I. Kitsuse, "Social Problems: A Re-Formulation," *Social Problems* 21, no. 2 (Fall 1973): 146, 147.

12. The term "recurring maintenance" derives from Jack L. Walker's typology of U.S. Senate agenda items ("Setting the Agenda in the U.S. Senate," p. 425).

13. Peter Bachrach and Morton S. Barratz, "Decisions and Non-Decisions: An Analytical Framework," *American Political Science Review* 57, no. 3 (September 1963): 632–642.

14. Anthony J. Proscio, "A Pernicious Charity: Being an Inquiry into How the Most Complicated Decisions Become Simple When You Know How They Turn Out" (Princeton, N.J.: Woodrow Wilson School, Princeton University, May 26, 1977), Xerox.

15. This discussion is based in part on the work of Cobb and Elder, *Participation in American Politics*, pp. 84–85. They add the category of unanticipated human events "such as a spontaneous riot [or] assassination" (p. 84), but that category seems to be subsumable under catastrophes. Bureaucratic motives for issue finding are not discussed, however. See also Campbell, "The Old People Boom and Japanese Policy Making."

16. Neil Smelser, *Theory of Collective Behavior* (New York: Free Press, 1962).

17. Anthony Downs, "Up and Down with Ecology—'The Issue Attention Cycle'," *Public Interest* 32 (Summer 1972): 38–50. See also Mark V. Nadel, "Consumer Protection Becomes a Public Issue (Again)," in James E. Anderson, ed., *Cases in Public Policy Making* (New York: Praeger, 1976), pp. 22–34; and P. F. Lazersfeld and Robert K. Merton, "Mass Communication, Popular Taste, and Organized Social Action," in W. Schramm and D. F. Roberts, eds., *The Process and Effects of Mass Communication* (Urbana, Ill.: University of Illinois Press, 1971), pp. 554–578.

18. Cobb et al., "Agenda Building," p. 127.

19. Raymond A. Bauer, Ithiel de Sola Pool, and Lewis Anthony Dexter, *American Business and Public Policy: The Politics of Foreign Trade* (New York: Atherton, 1963); Theodore J. Lowi, "American Business, Public Policy, Case Studies, and Political Theory," *World Politics* 16 (1964): 677–715; Theodore J. Lowi, *The End of Liberalism: Ideology, Policy, and the Crisis of Public Authority* (New York: Norton, 1969); Lewis A. Froman, Jr., "The Categorization of Policy Contents," in Austin Ranney, ed., *Political Science and Public Policy* (Chicago: Markham, 1968), pp. 41–52; E. E. Schattschneider, *Politics, Pressures, and the Tariff: A Study of Free Enterprise in Pressure Politics as Shown in the 1929–1930 Revision of the Tariff* (New York: Prentice-Hall, 1935); E. E. Schattschneider, *The Semi-Sovereign People* (New York: Holt, Rinehart and Winston, 1960); Robert H. Salisbury, "An Exchange Theory of Interest Groups," *Midwest Journal of Political Science* 8 (1969): 1–32; and Robert H. Salisbury and John P. Heinz, "A Theory of Policy Analysis and Some Preliminary Applications," in Ira Sharkansky, ed., *Policy Analysis in Political Science* (Chicago: Markham, 1970), pp. 39–60.

20. Michael T. Hayes, *Lobbyists and Legislators: A Theory of Political Markets* (New Brunswick, N.J.: Rutgers University Press, 1981), pp. 19–39.

21. Ibid., p. 31.

22. Angus Campbell et al., *Elections and the Political Order* (New York: Wiley, 1966), pp. 170–174.

23. Nick Kotz, *Let Them Eat Promises: The Politics of Hunger in America* (Englewood Cliffs, N.J.: Prentice-Hall, 1969).

24. David Mayhew, *Congress: The Electoral Connection* (New Haven: Yale University Press, 1974), p. 117, fn. 72. Mayhew is referring to the study by Donald S. Lutz and Richard W. Murray, "Coalition Formation in the Texas Legislature: Issues Payoffs and Winning Coalition Size," paper presented at the Midwest Political Science Association, 1972, pp. 11, 28. See also the article by the same name in *The Western Political Quarterly* 28, no. 2 (June 1975): 308–9.

25. Thomas E. Borcherding, "One Hundred Years of Public Spending in the United States" and "The Sources of Growth of Public Expenditures in the United States, 1902–1970," in Thomas E. Borcherding, ed., *Budgets and Bureaucrats: Sources of Government Growth* (Durham, N.C.: Duke University Press, 1977), pp. 19–44, 45–70.

26. Daniel Tarschys, "The Growth of Public Expenditures: Nine Modes of Explanations," in *Scandinavian Political Studies* 10 (1975): 9–31.

27. Borcherding, "The Sources of Growth."

28. James M. Buchanan, *The Limits of Liberty: Between Anarchy and Leviathan* (Chicago: University of Chicago Press, 1975), pp. 154–155.

29. Arthur M. Okun, *Equality and Efficiency: The Big Tradeoff* (Washington, D.C.: The Brookings Institution, 1975), pp. 2–3, and passim.

30. James M. Buchanan and Richard E. Wagner, *Democracy in Deficit: The Political Legacy of Lord Keynes* (New York: Academic Press, 1977).

31. Albert O. Hirschman makes a similar argument at the systemic level when he compares the economist's passion for "exit" (taking your business elsewhere) to the political scientist's interest in "voice" (institutional participation) as strategies for change. See Albert O. Hirschman, *Exit, Voice, and Loyalty* (Cambridge, Mass.: Harvard University Press, 1970).

32. Dahlerup, "The Socialization of Politics," p. 2; my emphasis.

Chapter 3

1. The importance of administrators in crafting social policy, especially in articulating the boundaries and directions of new issues of social policy, is well documented (but perhaps not well known by political scientists). Martha Derthick's comprehensive study, *Policymaking for Social Security* (Washington: The Brookings Institution, 1979) is perhaps the best demonstration of this phenomenon in America. From its inception, Social Security policy was the province of a small band of insiders, a practice which endured for forty years. The European research in this area is better known: Hugh Heclo, *Modern Social Policies in Britain and Sweden: From Relief to Income Maintenance* (New Haven: Yale University Press, 1974), pp. 301–303; and Ezra N. Suleiman, *Politics, Power, and Bureaucracy in France: The Administrative Elite* (Princeton, N.J.: Princeton University Press, 1974). For a recent comparative perspective, see Joel D. Aberbach, Robert D. Putnam, and Bert A. Rockman, with others, *Bureaucrats and Politicians in Western Democracies* (Cambridge, Mass.: Harvard University Press, 1981), pp. 134–149.

2. Nancy Pottishman Weiss, "Mother, the Invention of Necessity: Dr. Benjamin Spock's *Baby and Child Care*," *American Quarterly* 29 (Winter 1977): 520, fn. 3.

3. United States Department of Health, Education, and Welfare, Social Security Administration, Children's Bureau, "Your Children's Bureau" (Washington, D.C.: U.S. Government Printing Office, 1956).

4. Ibid., pp. ii, iv.

5. R. L. Duffus, *Lillian Wald: Neighbor and Crusader* (New York: The Macmillan Co., 1939), pp. 93–104, esp. pp. 93–95.

6. Edmund Morris, *The Rise of Theodore Roosevelt* (New York: Coward, McCann, and Geoghegan, Inc., 1979), pp. 34–35.

7. Florence Kelley, *Some Ethical Gains Through Legislation* (New York: The Macmillan Co., 1905), pp. 99–104.

8. Walter I. Trather, *From Poor Law to Welfare State* (New York: The Free Press, 1974), p. 182.

9. The description of Lathrop's decisions comes mainly from Jacqueline K. Parker and Edward M. Carpenter, "Julia Lathrop and the Children's Bureau: The Emergence of an Institution," *Social Service Review* 55, no. 1 (March 1981): 60–77.

10. Memorandum, Folks to Lathrop, May 15, 1912, RG 102, file 9-1-02, in Parker and Carpenter, p. 64.

11. Kelley, *Some Ethical Gains*, pp. 3–57.

12. James A. Tokey, *The Children's Bureau Today: Its History, Activities and Organization* (Baltimore: The Johns Hopkins Press, 1925), p. 153. See also "Birth Registration," U.S. Department of Commerce and Labor, Children's Bureau, Monograph no. 1 (Washington, D.C.: USGPO, 1933) and Parker and Carpenter, pp. 65–66.

13. The Children's Bureau was moved from the Department of Commerce and Labor to the Department of Labor in 1913, when the latter was established.

14. Susan Ware, *Beyond Suffrage: Women in the New Deal* (Cambridge: Harvard University Press, 1981), pp. 11, 14–36, 29, 33.

15. Gilbert Y. Steiner, *The Children's Cause* (Washington, D.C.: The Brookings Institution, 1976), pp. 37–38.

16. For a detailed description of these events, see "The Transfer of the Children's Bureau," in Harold Stein, ed., *Public Administration and Policy Development: A Casebook* (New York: Harcourt, Brace and Co., 1952), pp. 17–29.

17. Rachel Nyswander and Janet Hooks, "Employment of Women in the Federal Government, 1923–1939," *Women's Bulletin* no. 182 (Washington, 1941), p. 5; in Ware, *Beyond Suffrage*, p. 21.

18. Steiner, *The Children's Cause*, p. 40.

19. "Reorganization of the Children's Bureau," memorandum from Mary E. Switzer to HEW Secretary Robert Finch (Jan. 30, 1969) in Steiner, *The Children's Cause*, p. 41.

20. Aberbach and Rockman have shown that the upper echelons of civil servants in HEW were distinctly Democratic in partisanship and committed to the Democratic norms of federal presence in social programs. See Joel D. Aberbach and Bert A. Rockman, "Clashing Belief Systems within the Executive Branch: The Nixon Administration Bureaucracy," *American Political Science Review* 70 (June 1976): 456–468.

21. Barbara J. Nelson, "Purchase of Services," in George Washnis, ed., *Productivity Handbook for State and Local Government* (New York: John Wiley and Sons, 1980), p. 446, fn. 34.

22. Vincent De Francis, *Child Protective Services in the United States: Reporting a Nationwide Survey* (Denver: Children's Division, the American Humane Association, 1956), p. 7.

23. Children's Bureau, *Annual Report*, (unpublished), fiscal year 1956 p. III, 10–11.

24. For a discussion of the debates of the scope and direction of social services in this period, see Charles E. Gilbert, "Policy Making in Public Welfare: The 1962 Amendments," *Political Science Quarterly* 81, no. 2 (June 1966): 196–224.

25. See, for example, Norma D. Feshbach and Seymeur Feshbach, "Toward an Historical, Social and Developmental Perspective on Children's Rights," *Journal of Social Issues* 25, no. 2 (1978): 1–7; and C. R. Margolin, "Salvation Versus Liberation: The Movement for Children's Rights in 'Historical Context'," *Social Problems* 25, no. 4 (April 1978): 441–452.

26. Children's Bureau, *Annual Report*, unpublished, fiscal year 1960, p. III-84; my emphasis, except for "Ohio," which was emphasized in the original.

27. Children's Bureau, *Annual Report*, unpublished, fiscal year 1961, p. V-142.

28. Children's Bureau, *Annual Report*, unpublished, fiscal year 1962, p. III-59.

29. Ibid., p. 60.

30. For a review of the diffusion of innovation literature, see Lawrence A. Brown, *Innovation Diffusion: A New Perspective* (London: Methuen, 1981), pp. 3–10.

31. See, for examples, Children's Bureau, *Annual Report*, unpublished, fiscal years 1961–65 and 1967.

32. Kempe et al., "The Battered-Child Syndrome."

33. David G. Gil, *Violence against Children*.

34. Presently child welfare services are funded under Title IVB of the Social Security Act.

35. *Report on the Advisory Council on Child Welfare Services*, U.S. Department of Health, Education, and Welfare, Social Security Administration, December 28, 1959 (Washington, D.C.: U.S. Government Printing Office, 1960), p. 10.

36. Public Law 86-778, September 13, 1960, Sec. 526 (a). The sum was not fixed by law. See the *Appendix to the Budget for Fiscal Year 1962*, p. 677, which shows that the first grant became available in fiscal year 1962.

37. Budget figures derived from the *Appendix to the Budget for Fiscal Years 1964*, and *1968*, pp. 466, 467, and pp. 491, 492, respectively. Fiscal year 1964 and 1968 are used because actual expenditures are available from the budget figures in the N + 2 fiscal year. As the text describes, admin-

istrative reorganization removed the Children's Bureau from the Welfare Administration to the Social and Rehabilitative Services Administration in 1967, disrupting internal record keeping. Changes in the budget format recommended by President Lyndon Johnson's Commission on Budget Concepts and implemented by President Nixon make comparisons in actual expenditures impossible after fiscal year 1966. For a description of the consequences of the changes in the budget, see David J. Ott and Attiat F. Ott, *Federal Budget Policy* (Washington, D.C.: The Brookings Institution, 1977, third edition).

38. The 1963 Maternal and Child Health and Mental Retardation Planning Amendments to the Social Security Act provided for research funds on maternal and child health and crippled children problems which paralleled the child welfare research sections of the 1960 amendments. See Public Law 88-156, October 24, 1963, Part 4, Sec. 532 (a).

39. The budget figures are *not* in constant dollars. Personnel and expenditure figures are drawn from the *Appendix to the Budget of the United States for the Fiscal Year Ending on June 30, 1962* (for fiscal year 1960 figures) and the same for Fiscal Year *1968* (for fiscal year 1968 figures). The fiscal year 1968 figures are estimates; see note 37 for a description of budget reporting changes which make the use of estimated figures necessary for that year.

40. Laurence E. Lynn, Jr., and David deF. Whitman, *The President as Policy Maker* (Philadelphia: Temple University Press, 1981), pp. 58–89; Gilbert Y. Steiner, *The State of Welfare* (Washington, D.C.: The Brookings Institution, 1971), pp. 1–30; Rufus E. Miles, Jr., *The Department of H.E.W.* (New York: Praeger, 1974); and Joseph Califano, *Governing America* (New York: Simon and Schuster, 1981), pp. 41–48.

41. The first five chiefs of the Children's Bureau were women: Julia Lathrop (1912–1921), Grace Abbott (1921–1934), Katherine Lenroot (1934–1949), Martha Eliot (1949–1957), and Katherine Oettinger (1957–1968). The first four chiefs were not married (and had no children). Secretary of HEW Marion B. Folsom, who conducted the search to find a successor to Dr. Eliot, felt there were political problems in having the Children's Bureau headed by a childless woman. The implicit qualifications changed. Katherine Oettinger, who was chosen for the job, described it this way: "He [Folsom] said it should not only be a woman but should be a woman who has been a mother and so he added that to the qualifications; a bit unfair, I think, but he had a feeling that it was a plus quality, so he sent out an alarm to all the agencies. . . ."

Chapter 4

1. Anthony Downs, "Up and Down with Ecology—'The Issue Attention Cycle'," *Public Interest* 32 (Summer 1972): 38–50.

2. Ibid. See also Mark V. Nadel, "Consumer Protection Becomes a Public Issue (Again)," in James E. Anderson, ed., *Cases in Public Policy Making*

(New York: Praeger, 1976), pp. 22–34; and P. F. Lazersfeld and Robert K. Merton, "Mass Communication, Popular Taste, and Organized Social Action," in W. Schramm and D. F. Roberts, eds., *The Process and Effects of Mass Communication* (Urbana, Ill.: University of Illinois Press, 1971), pp. 554–578.

3. Tom Wilkinson, "Covering Abuse: Context and Policy—Gaining Access," in George Gerbner, Catherine J. Ross, and Edward Zigler, eds., *Child Abuse: An Agenda for Action* (New York: Oxford University Press, 1980), p. 250.

4. Leon V. Sigal, "Newsmen and Campaigners: Organization Men Make the News," *Political Science Quarterly* 93, no. 3 (Fall 1978): 465.

5. Arthur H. Miller, Edie N. Goldenberg, and Lutz Erbring, "Type-Set Politics: Impact of Newspapers on Public Confidence," *The American Political Science Review* 73, no. 1 (March 1979): 67–86.

6. Downs, "Up and Down," p. 39.

7. Ibid., p. 39.

8. In recounting the public's introduction to the problem we depend heavily on the accounts of the Mary Ellen case carried in the *New York Times*. This is a decision based on the exigencies of research, not on the *Times*'s stature during that period. In the 1870s, the *Times* was one of the smallest New York dailies; it certainly was not the "newspaper of record" it is today. More to the point, however, is the fact that an index to the *New York Times* articles, and often editorials, is available from 1851 on. The *Index* is not only useful in guiding researchers to their topics of interest, but also constitutes a unique statement of what problems contemporary observers thought were important and how those problems were labeled. (Information on the *New York Times Index* comes from the forewords of the 1851–1862, 1863–1874, and 1905–1906 editions of the *Index* as well as the entry on the *New York Times Index* in the *Guide to Reference Books*, compiled by Gene Sheehy [Chicago: American Library Association, 1976], p. 188. The two periods when contemporary indexing was not done were back-indexed. The date when the back-indexing began is not given; however, the first copyright of a back-indexed volume was issued in 1967. The forewords to the back-indexed volumes state that the back-indexing tried to conform in topic and tone to the contemporary indexes nearest those dates.)

9. Michael Schudson, *Discovering the News: A Social History of American Newspapers* (New York: Basic Books, 1978), p. 112.

10. The *New York Times*, April 10, 1874, p. 8.

11. The *New York Times*, December 29, 1874, p. 2.

12. Judy Walkowitz argues that British reform women often identified with the women they sought to help, but men did not. In our case, SPCCs were dominated by men, and sympathy toward clients never took hold. See Judy Walkowitz, *Prostitution and Victorian Society* (Cambridge: Cambridge University Press, 1980), pp. 6–7, 138.

13. C. Henry Kempe et al., "The Battered-Child Syndrome," pp. 17–24.

14. The figures reported here were derived by summing the articles listed under the appropriate headings in the following indexes. For the professional media: *Index Medicus*, the *Index of Legal Periodicals*, the *Social Science Index*, the *Humanities Index*, and the *Education Index*. Figures for mass-circulation magazines derived from the *Readers' Guide to Periodical Literature*. No reductions were made for the possiblity of double counting.

15. For two perspectives on television's response to child abuse and other social problems, see Donn H. O'Brien, Alfred R. Schneider, and Herminio Tratiesas, "Portraying Abuse: Network Censors' Round Table"; and George Gerbner, "Children and Power on Television: The Other Side of the Picture," in Gerbner et al., *Child Abuse*, pp. 231–238, 239–248.

16. For research on the association between illegitimacy and abuse, see Ellen C. Herrenkohl and Ron C. Herrenkohl, "Comparison of Abused Children and Their Non-Abused Siblings," *Journal of the American Academy of Child Psychiatry* 18, no. 2 (Spring 1979): 260–269. For research on abuse in military families, see Marilyn Allen, "Child Maltreatment in Military Communities," *Juvenile Justice* 26, no. 2 (May 1975): 11–20.

17. Children who "battered" their parents have increasingly drawn popular interest. The British journal, *The Economist*, carried an article called "Battered Parents" on November 19, 1977 (pp. 25–26). On Saturday, April 16, 1980, Tom Snyder reported on "Children Abusing Adults" during the NBC News Program *Prime Time Saturday*. Two months later, ABC picked up on a similar topic. On June 11, 1980, ABC's *World News Tonight* included a report on abuse of the elderly.

18. U.S. Children's Bureau, *Annual Report*, fiscal year 1960, unpublished, p. III-84.

19. P. N. Woolley and William A. Evans, Jr., "Significance of Skeletal Lesions in Infants Resembling Those of Traumatic Origins," *Journal of the American Medical Association* 158, no. 7 (June 18, 1955): 539–543.

20. Ibid., p. 540.

21. Stephen J. Phohl, "The 'Discovery' of Child Abuse," *Social Problems* 24, no. 3 (February 1977): 315–318.

22. American Medical Association, "Parental Abuse Looms in Childhood Deaths," news release, July 13, 1962.

23. "The Battered-Child Syndrome," editorial in the *Journal of the American Medical Association* 181, no. 1 (July 7, 1962), p. 42.

24. "When They're Angry . . . ," *Newsweek*, April 16, 1962, p. 74; and "Battered Child Syndrome," *Time*, July 20, 1962, p. 60.

25. Charles Flato, "Parents Who Beat Children: A Tragic Increase in Cases of Child Abuse is Prompting a Hunt for Ways to Select Sick Adults Who Commit Such Crimes," *The Saturday Evening Post*, October 6, 1962, pp. 32–35.

26. Ibid., p. 32.

27. Ibid., p. 35.

28. See note 14 above for a description of the counting procedures.

29. In 1960, *Index Medicus*, the *Index to Legal Periodicals*, the *Education Index*, and the *International Index* (later to become the *Social Science and Humanities Index*) combined indexed articles from 2,305 journals. (Double entries are *not* eliminated; this figure is the sum of the journals listed in each index.) In 1970, these references indexed 3,096 journals and in 1980, 3,614 journals. Over the same period the *Readers' Guide to Periodical Literature* grew from indexing 110 journals (1960), to 162 journals (1970), to 184 journals (1980).

30. Vincent De Francis, "Child Abuse Legislation: Analysis of Mandatory Reporting Laws in the United States" (Denver: Children's Division, the American Humane Association, 1966), p. 1.

31. Harrison Salisbury, *Without Fear or Favor: The New York Times and Our Times* (New York: Time Books, 1980), pp. 558–560.

32. Joseph R. Dominick, "Crime and Law Enforcement in the Mass Media," in Charles Winick, ed., *Deviance and Mass Media* (Beverly Hills, Cal.: Sage, 1978), p. 108.

33. Gans's research on the content of the CBS and NBC nightly news and the news magazines *Time* and *Newsweek* shows that crime-and-victim news also forms a steady part of news offerings in these outlets. Roughly 7% of the stories or columns from these news sources were devoted to alleged or actual lawbreakers or their victims, a substantial percentage especially for television news, which is often castigated for being merely a "headline service." Herbert Gans, *Deciding What's News* (New York: Pantheon, 1979), p. 13 from table 3: "Unknowns in the News." The figure is derived from an unweighted average of all four news outlets for the three years under study—1967, 1971, and 1975. The figure assumes that approximately 20% of news from these sources is about relatively "unknown" people (p. 13).

34. "Kingdom and Cabbage," *Time*, August 15, 1977, p. 75.

35. The *New York Times*, February 9, 1873, p. 6.

36. Ibid., February 11, 1873, p. 8.

37. Ibid., April 11, 1874, p. 2.

38. Ibid., December 27, 1874, p. 12.

39. For a description of the "unnatural mother as abuser," see Edward Zigler, "Controlling Child Abuse in America: An Effort Doomed to Failure?" in Richard Bourne and Eli H. Newberger, eds., *Critical Perspectives on Child Abuse* (Lexington, Mass.: Lexington Books, 1979), pp. 171–214.

40. It is interesting to note that between 1954 and 1967, when a separate file on child abuse was added, more than half of the child welfare articles saved dealt with child abuse. Stories covering Aid to Dependent Children and welfare fraud comprise the second largest group. Ironically, the term "abuse" occurs most frequently in the articles on ADC, where reporting

reflects a dual concern for maintaining strict control over proper payments and encouraging work incentives.

41. "Assembly to Sift Child Beating Bill," *Trenton Evening Times*, April 13, 1964. See also John T. McGowan, "House Votes Bill on Child Beating," *Newark Evening News*, April 14, 1964, p. 17. Most of the articles reporting the Espinoza and Tabor cases cannot be paginated. They derive from the clipping file of the New Jersey State Library, which dated them and noted the newspaper. Archives for the relevant newspapers do not exist for this period.

42. "Police Say Child Was Shackled; Mother in Jail," *Philadelphia Inquirer*, April 28, 1964.

43. Ibid.

44. David A. Jewell, "Welfare Aid Defends Ruling in Tragic Case," *Philadelphia Inquirer*, April 29, 1964.

45. "Child Welfare Aide Defends Staff," *Trenton Evening Times*, April 29, 1964, p. 22.

46. David A. Jewell, "Mother Cited in Child-Beating Denies She's Unfit," *Philadelphia Inquirer*, June 28, 1964, p. 1, New Jersey Section.

47. Gans, *Deciding What's News*, pp. 203–206; and Schudson, *Discovering*, pp. 77–87.

48. David G. Gil, *Violence against Children* (Cambridge, Mass.: The Harvard University Press, 1973), p. 61, table 5: "Sources of Respondent's Knowledge of the General Problem of Child Abuse during the Year Preceding the Survey." Respondents could mention more than one source.

49. Ibid., p. 66, table 10: "What Respondents Thought Should be Done About Perpetrators of Child Abuse."

50. Gaye Tuchman, "Making News by Doing Work: Routinizing the Unexpected," *American Journal of Sociology* 79, no. 1 (July 1973): 114.

51. Helen MacGill Hughes, *News and the Human Interest Story* (Chicago: University of Chicago Press, 1940), p. 58.

Chapter 5

1. Jack L. Walker, "The Diffusion of Innovations among the American States," *American Political Science Review* 63 (September 1969): 895.

2. The only article to consider child abuse reporting laws as an example of diffusion of innovation is Barbara J. Nelson with the assistance of Thomas Lindenfeld, "Setting the Public Agenda: The Case of Child Abuse," in Judith V. May and Aaron Wildavsky, eds., *The Policy Cycle* (Beverly Hills: Sage, 1978), pp. 17–41.

3. Robert Eyestone, "Confusion, Diffusion and Innovation," *American Political Science Review* 71 (June 1977): 441.

4. Everett Rogers and F. Floyd Shoemaker, *Communication of Innovations: A Cross-Cultural Approach* (New York: Free Press, 1971), p. 19.

5. Eyestone, "Confusion," p. 442.

6. Ibid., p. 442.

7. To be technically accurate, the Children's Division of the AHA preferred calling their efforts "legislative guidelines," not a model statute.

8. Two studies have, however, considered the role of multiple cues in diffusion of innovation. See Irwin Feller and Donald C. Menzel, "Diffusion Milieus as a Focus of Research on Innovation in the Public Sector," *Policy Science* 8, no. 1 (March 1977): 49–68, esp. pp. 52–53; and Rogers and Shoemaker, *Communication*, p. 22.

9. Walker, "The Diffusion of Innovations," p. 895.

10. Earlier research reported that twenty-six state legislatures did not hold a regular session in 1966 (Nelson, "Setting the Public Agenda," p. 30). The change is due to reclassifying Wisconsin as having a regular session in 1966. See the *Book of the States*, 1968–69, p. 65.

11. Virginia Gray, "Innovation in the States: A Diffusion Study," *American Political Science Review* 67 (December 1973): 1175.

12. Other patterns of diffusion, notably long patterns, also fit some data. Likewise, the rapid phase of the S-curve has also been likened to the S-curve for learning, and learning-trial theory has also been applied. (Gray, "Innovation in the States," pp. 1195–96, and Eyestone, "Confusion," pp. 445–446.

13. See John L. Foster, "Regionalism and Innovation in the American States," *Journal of Politics* 40 (1978): 179–87; Walker, "The Diffusion of Innovations," p. 895; Minger and Feller, "Diffusion Milieus," p. 732. Research on elite networks supports the assumption that states do emulate each other. For example, Walker investigated the communication pattern of top administrators in the education, labor, mental health, and welfare departments, the budget bureaus, the legislative reference service, and the governor's chief assistant for program development, and found extensive communication with other states. The states are often, though not always, in the same geographical region. These findings led Walker to postulate a two-step diffusion-of-innovations process. First, national leaders adopt new legislation, then regional leaders adopt it, with the innovation then diffusing within regions. Several years later, Gray's research contradicted Walker's, asserting that "innovativeness is not a pervasive factor [for a state]; rather it is issue- and time-specific at best" (Gray, "Innovations in the States," p. 1185).

14. Alan Sussman and Stephen J. Cohen, "The Incidence of Child Neglect in the United States," in their *Reporting Child Abuse and Neglect* (Cambridge, Mass.: Ballinger, 1975), p. 125.

15. The term venturesome derives from Roger and Shoemaker, *Communication*, p. 183.

16. Walker, "The Diffusion of Innovation," p. 383; and George W. Downs, Jr., *Bureaucracy, Innovation, and Public Policy* (Lexington, Mass.: Lexington Books, 1976).

17. Gray, "Innovation in the States," p. 1184. See also Virginia Gray, "Expenditures and Innovations as Dimensions of 'Progressivism': A Note on the American States," *American Journal of Political Science* 18 (November 1974): 693–699.

18. Lawrence Mohr, "Determinants of Innovation in Organizations," *American Political Science Review* 63 (March 1969): 112.

19. Alan Rosenthal and Rod Forth, "There Ought to Be a Law!" *State Government* 51 (Spring 1978): 81–87.

20. Alan Rosenthal, "American State Legislatures Today: Their Role and Effectiveness," lecture given at Princeton University, October 12, 1978.

21. New Jersey P.L. 1880, c.XCV and New Jersey P.L. 1883, c.IV.

22. Jeanne M. Giovannoni and Rosina M. Becerra, *Defining Child Abuse* (New York: The Free Press, 1979), pp. 43, 61–66.

23. *First Conference on the Care of Dependent Children,* 1909, pp. 9–10, in Giovannoni and Beccera, *Defining Child Abuse,* p. 61.

24. New Jersey P.L. 1915, c. 246.

25. "Two City Social Agencies for Child Welfare Merge," *Newark News,* September 25, 1960, p. W 14.

26. In 1910, Mother's Aid came to New Jersey in an unusual fashion. The State Board of Children's Guardians asked the attorney general to rule that Mother's Aid "was within its legal powers." See James Leiby, *Charity and Correction in New Jersey* (New Brunswick, N.J.: Rutgers University Press, 1967), p. 94.

27. Dawes Thompson, "Child Neglect Law Changes Urged to Fight Delinquency," *Newark News,* January 31, 1957, p. 24.

28. Claire R. Hancock, "Protective Services and the Problem of Neglect of Children in New Jersey," *The Welfare Reporter* 10 (April 1959): 68–81.

29. New Jersey P.L. 1962 c. 197.

30. Leontine Young, *Wednesday's Children* (New York, McGraw-Hill, 1964). The book was based on her doctoral dissertation, "The Behavior Syndrome of Parents Who Neglect and Abuse Their Children," Columbia University, 1963.

31. "A Public Hearing before the New Jersey General Assembly Committee on Institutions, Public Health and Welfare on Assembly Bill No. 514 Providing for the Mandatory Reporting by Physicians of Physical Abuses of Children," New Jersey Assembly, March 26, 1964, pp. 3–5, 10–11 and 13.

32. Ibid., p. 35.

33. New Jersey P.L. 1971, c. 437.

34. New Jersey P.L. 1977, c. 210.

35. New Jersey Statutes Annotated (1953) 2A: 97-2.

36. New Jersey P.L. 1973, c. 147.

37. New Jersey P.L. 1974, c. 119 and New Jersey P.L. 1977, c. 209.

38. P.L. 92-247, Sect. 4(b) (2) (A–J).

39. Sanford N. Katz, Melba McGrath, Ruth-Arlene Howe, *Child Neglect Laws in America* (American Bar Association Section on Family Law, 1976); Institute of Judicial Administration—American Bar Association, Juvenile Justice Standards Project (IJA-ABA), *Standards Relating to Abuse and Neglect* (Cambridge, Mass.: Ballinger Publishing Co.; tentative draft 1977), p. 33. IJA-ABA Juvenile Justice Standards, 13 *Clearinghouse Review* 667 (1980); Robert Burt; IJA-ABA, *Juvenile Justice Standards Relating to Abuse and Neglect*, 1981; Alan Sussman and Stephan J. Cohen, *Reporting Child Abuse and Neglect: Guidelines for Legislation* (Cambridge, Mass.: Ballinger Publishing Co., 1975); and National Center on Child Abuse and Neglect, *Federal Standards for Child Abuse and Neglect Prevention and Treatment Programs and Projects* (Washington, D.C.: United States Children's Bureau, Administration for Children, Youth, and Families, Office of Human Development Services, Department of Health, Education, and Welfare, March 1978; draft for review purposes only).

40. Sussman and Cohen, *Reporting Child Abuse*, pp. 29–33; and Child Abuse and Neglect Project, "Child Abuse and Neglect: Model Legislation for the States" (Denver, Colo.: Education Commission of the States, March 1976, second printing, Report No. 71, pp. 23–24).

41. Interview with Susan Matthews, NJ-DYFS (14 July 1980).

42. See, for example, Katherine L. Armstrong, "How to Avoid Burnout: A Study of the Relationship between Burnout and Worker, Organizational and Management Characteristics in Eleven Abuse and Neglect Projects," *Child Abuse and Neglect* 3, no. 1 (1979): 145–149.

43. Michael Lipsky, *Street Level Bureaucracy* (New York: Russell Sage, 1980), pp. 133–139; and Barbara J. Nelson, "Client Evaluations of Social Programs," in Charles T. Goodsell, ed., *The Public Encounter: Where State and Citizen Meet* (Bloomington, Ind.: Indiana University Press, 1981), pp. 23–42.

44. Wald's cautious approach to state intervention covers dependency and abuse as well as neglect. See footnote 2 (and passim) in Michael S. Wald, "State Intervention on Behalf of 'Neglected' Children: Standards for Removal of Children from Their Homes, Monitoring of the Status of Children in Foster Care, and Termination of Parental Rights," *Stanford Law Review* 28 (April 1976): 625. See also Michael S. Wald, "State Intervention on Behalf of 'Neglected' Children: A Search for Realistic Standards," *Stanford Law Review* 27 (April 1975): 985–1040.

45. "Adoption Aid, Child Welfare," *Congressional Quarterly Almanac* (1980), p. 418.

46. Joseph Goldstein, Anna Freud, and Albert J. Solnit, *Before the Best Interests of the Child* (New York: Free Press, 1979), p. 72. Also referenced is Joseph Goldstein, Anna Freud, and Albert J. Solnit, *Beyond the Best Interests of the Child* (New York: Free Press, 1973).

47. Goldstein et al., *Before*, p. 9.

48. Stanley Z. Fisher, "Parents' Rights and Juvenile Court Jurisdiction: A Review of *Before the Best Interests of the Child*," *American Bar Foun-*

dation Research Journal (Summer 1981), no. 3, pp. 835–849; Michael S. Wald, "Thinking About Public Policy Toward Abuse and Neglect of Children: A Review of *Before the Best Interests of the Child*," vol. 78 (March 1980), pp. 645–693; and Milton Shore, "Book Review of *Before the Best Interests of the Child*," *Journal of Marriage and the Family* 43, no. 3 (August 1981): 749–50.

49. Fisher, "Parents' Rights," p. 838.

50. *Santosky v. Kramer* 455 U.S. 745.

Chapter 6

1. Membership on the District of Columbia Committee in either house blocks a member from meeting the four main goals of office holding: wielding institutional power, crafting public policy, promoting reelection, or grooming oneself for other careers. See Richard F. Fenno, Jr., *Congressmen in Committees* (Boston: Little, Brown and Co., 1973), p. 139; A. Robert Smith, *The Tiger in the Senate* (New York: Doubleday, 1962), pp. 179–187; and Ralph K. Huitt and Robert L. Peabody, *Congress: Two Decades of Analysis* (New York: Harper and Row, 1969), pp. 113–135. Recently, however, some black members of Congress have felt that service on the D.C. Committees is a platform for discussing a variety of racial and urban issues.

2. Gary Orfield notes that the period between 1965 and 1975 saw extraordinary congressional initiatives in social policy. During the Nixon presidency this was allowed in part because Nixon did not come to the White House with a fixed domestic agenda and spent little time on social issues except "to slow down civil rights enforcement and become tougher on crime." Gary Orfield, *Congressional Power: Congress and Social Change* (New York: Harcourt, Brace, Jovanovich, 1975), p. 55 and passim. In other words, for social policy issues, Nixon *reacted* to a liberal Congress.

3. David E. Price, "Policy Making in Congressional Committees: The Impact of Environmental Factors," *American Political Science Review* 72, no. 2 (June 1978): 548, 574.

4. John R. Johannes, *Policy Innovation in Congress* (Morristown, N.J.: General Learning Press, 1972), p. 280.

5. Ibid., p. 282, fn. 6.

6. Nelson W. Polsby, "Policy Analysis and Congress," *Public Policy* 18 (Fall 1969): 64, 65; my emphasis.

7. David R. Mayhew, *Congress: The Electoral Connection* (New Haven, Conn.: Yale University Press, 1974, 1976), p. 95.

8. Norman Ornstein, Robert L. Peabody, and David W. Rohde, "The Changing Senate: From the 1950s to the 1970s" in Lawrence C. Dodd and Bruce I. Oppenheimer, eds., *Congress Reconsidered* (New York: Praeger, 1977), pp. 3–20.

9. Eric M. Uslaner, "The Case of the Vanishing Liberal Senators: The House Did It," *British Journal of Political Science* 11 (January 1981): 106.

10. John Manley, *The Politics of Finance* (Boston: Little, Brown, 1970), p. 21.

11. Fenno, *Congressmen*, p. 140; and Price, "Policy Making," p. 334.

12. Fenno, *Congressmen*, p. 226.

13. *Congressional Record*, July 14, 1973, p. 23901.

14. During the 1970s the "new" Tenth Congressional District included the "east Bronx and the northern fringes of Queens." See Michael Barone, Grant Ujifusa, and Douglas Matthews, *The Almanac of American Politics 1980* (New York: E. P. Dutton, 1979), p. 593 and passim.

15. *Congressional Record*, July 14, 1973, p. 23901.

16. Ellen Hoffman, "Policy and Politics: The Child Abuse Prevention and Treatment Act," *Public Policy* 26, no. 1 (Winter 1978): 72.

17. Ibid. For a more general discussion of the role of constituents in setting the congressional agenda, see John W. Kingdon, "Dynamics of Agenda Formulation in Congress," in James E. Anderson, ed., *Cases in Public Policy Making* (New York: Praeger, 1976), pp. 37–38.

18. The quotation is from the text of the president's veto message (H. Doc. 92-48) as contained in the *Congressional Record*, daily edition, December 10, 1971, pp. S 21129–30, as cited in Gilbert Y. Steiner, *The Children's Cause* (Washington, D.C.: The Brookings Institution, 1976), p. 113.

19. The reference to "recommendation" comes from Harold D. Lasswell, "The Decision Process: Seven Categories of Functional Analysis," in Nelson W. Polsby, Robert A. Dentler, and Paul A. Smith, eds., *Politics and Social Life: An Introduction to Political Behavior* (Boston: Houghton Mifflin Co., 1963), pp. 93–105.

20. Hoffman, "Policy and Politics," p. 75.

21. "Child Abuse Prevention Act, 1973," p. 25; *Hearings before the Subcommittee on Children and Youth of the Committee on Labor and Public Welfare*, U.S. Senate, Ninety-third Congress, First Session, p. 50. Hereafter cited as the Senate Hearing, March, 1973.

22. Ibid., p. 59.

23. Joan Barthel, "A Cruel Inheritance," *Life*, June 1979, vol. 2, no. 6, pp. 73–82.

24. Hoffman, "Policy and Politics," p. 86.

25. Senate Hearing, March 1973, p. 158.

26. Ibid., p. 293.

27. Ibid., pp. 17, 18.

28. Ibid., p. 13; my emphasis.

29. Ibid., p. 43.

30. U.S. House of Representatives, Committee on Education and Labor, "Report on the Child Abuse Prevention and Treatment Act, together with Dissenting Views," November 30, 1973, Report No. 93-685, Ninety-third Congress, First Session, p. 12.

31. Martha Derthick, *Uncontrollable Spending for Social Services Grants* (Washington, D.C.: Brookings Institution, 1975), p. 2.

32. Senate Hearing, March 1973, p. 91.

33. Ibid., p. 89.

34. Ibid.

35. Ibid., p. 94.

36. Hoffman, "Policy and Politics," p. 81.

37. *Congressional Record*, July 14, 1973, p. 23905.

38. Hoffman, "Policy and Politics," p. 80.

39. *Congressional Record*, July 14, 1973, p. 23904.

40. Even in the early days of congressional efforts to respond to child abuse, Congresswoman Schroeder saw the larger picture. She understood that sexual abuse was an important aspect of child abuse long before such connections were commonly recognized. Very early she considered proposing a "Family Violence Act," although later domestic violence legislation was technically outside her purview.

41. "To Establish a National Center on Child Abuse and Neglect," *Hearings before the Select Subcommittee on Education of the Committee on Education and Labor;* U.S. Congress, House of Representatives, Ninety-third Congress, First Session, 1974 (hereafter cited as the "1973 House Hearings"), pp. 151–152. (The hearings took place in 1973, although the transcription was not published until 1974.)

42. Lunsford's position paper was concerned with proposed changes in the Social Security Act which the League felt would downgrade protective services in general.

43. Hoffman, "Policy and Politics," pp. 79–80.

44. House Hearings, 1973, pp. 96, 97.

45. Hoffman, "Policy and Politics," p. 82.

46. *Congressional Record*, December 3, 1973, p. 39227.

47. Mandating the criteria of state reporting laws and tying certain grants to fulfilling those criteria (a classic example of carrot-and-stick federalism) proved to be a real sticking point in states like Colorado which had good services, an imperfect reporting law, and an intractable state legislature unwilling to change the law.

48. Jack L. Walker, "Setting the Agenda in the U.S. Senate: A Theory of Problem Selection," *British Journal of Political Science* 7 (October 1977): 425.

49. Cranston was more successful two years later. In June of 1980, Congress passed, and President Carter signed, the Adoption Assistance and Child Welfare Act in an effort to limit state reliance on foster care and to spur permanent adoptions for needy children. The act authorized federal matching for state spending on foster care (with a conditional expenditure ceiling) and required states to establish programs to assist families who wanted to adopt children with "special needs" (i.e., handicaps).

50. JoAnn Gaspar, "Beating Up on the Family," *Conservative Digest*, March, 1980, p. 36.

51. Sec. 610 (a) (1) *Omnibus Budget Reconciliation Act of 1981, No. 1*, House of Representatives Report No. 97-208, Ninety-seventh Congress, First Session, July 29, 1981, p. 765.

52. On September 1, 1981, Assistant Secretary for Human Development Services Dorcas Hardy wrote a memorandum to the Budget Task Force and others saying: "I would like to amend my FY 1983 budget request by deleting the categorical funding for the service grant programs under Child Abuse and Neglect and Developmental Disabilities."

53. John Ellwood et al., "Background Material on Fiscal Year 1982 Federal Budget Reductions" (Princeton, N.J.: Princeton Urban and Regional Research Center, Woodrow Wilson School, Princeton University, March 1982), p. 6. See also Joel Haveman, *Congress and the Budget* (Bloomington, Ind.: Indiana University Press, 1978).

54. Allen Schick, "Reconciliation and the Congressional Budget Process" (Washington, D.C.: American Enterprise Institute, Congress Project, May 20, 1981), p. 38.

55. For a review of congressional response to issues of child welfare and "violent deviance," see Gilbert Y. Steiner, *The Futility of Family Policy* (Washington, D.C.: The Brookings Institution, 1981); and the following articles from the *Congressional Quarterly Almanac*: "Subcommittee Approves Criminal Law Reform" (on changes in the rape laws) (1975, pp. 541–552); "Congress Overrides Health Services Veto" (on the establishment of the National Center for the Prevention and Control of Rape in NIMH) (1975, pp. 591–601); "Day Care Center Staffing" (Child and Family Services Act) (1975, pp. 691–693); "Major Health Programs Extended" (National Center for the Prevention and Control of Rape in NIMH) (1977, pp. 453–455); "Finance Committee Shapes Welfare Bill" (Carter Welfare Reform) (1977, pp. 511–514); "Adoption, Child Welfare" (1977, pp. 514–515); "Child Abuse Adoption" (1977, pp. 508–510); "Child Pornography" (1977, pp. 520–523); "Child Abuse, Adoption Act" (1978, pp. 599–600); "Rape Victim Privacy" (1978, p. 196); "Domestic Violence" (1978, p. 580); "Child Pornography" (1978, p. 582); "Senate-Passed Criminal Code Dies in House," (See chapter 16: Rape Criminal Code Reform) (1978, pp. 165–173); "House Passes Child Health Assurance Bill" (1979, pp. 499–504); "Adoption Aid, Child Welfare" (1979, pp. 529–532); "Domestic Violence" (1979, pp. 508–509); "Adoption Aid, Child Welfare" (1980, pp. 417–418); "Expanded Mental Health Services Approved" (rape services) (1980, pp. 430–434); and "Conservatives Kill Domestic Violence Bill" (1980, pp. 443–445).

56. Richard B. Dingman, "The Future: Focus on Domestic Family Issues under President Reagan and the New Congress," speech given at Princeton University, November 11, 1980.

Chapter 7

1. See Lester C. Thurow, *The Zero-Sum Society* (New York: Basic Books, 1980).

2. See "$2 million set for funding up to 20 Child Abuse and Neglect R & D Projects," *Child Protection Report* 8, no. 9 (May 7, 1982): 3–4.

3. Anthony Downs, "Up and Down with Ecology—The 'Issue-Attention' Cycle," *Public Interest* 28 (Summer 1972): 39–41.

4. "Kingdom and Cabbage," *Time*, August 15, 1977, p. 75.

5. Murray Straus, Richard J. Gelles, and Suzanne K. Steinmetz, *Behind Closed Doors: Violence in the American Family* (New York: Anchor, 1980), pp. 147–152; Leroy H. Pelton, "Child Abuse and Neglect: The Myth of Classlessness," in Leroy H. Pelton, ed., *The Social Context of Child Abuse and Neglect* (New York: Human Sciences Press, 1981), pp. 23–38; and Richard J. Light, "Abused and Neglected Children in America: A Study of Alternative Policies," *Harvard Educational Review* 43 (November 1973): 556–598.

6. Sheila Rule, "City Concerned as Reports Rise on Child Abuse," The *New York Times*, September 30, 1981, p. B1.

7. Jack L. Walker, "Diffusion of Innovations Among American States," *American Political Science Review* 63 (September 1969): 895.

8. Michael S. Wald, "State Intervention on Behalf of 'Neglected' Children: Standards for Removal of Children from Their Homes, Monitoring the Status of Children in Foster Care, and Termination of Parental Rights," *Stanford Law Review* 28 (April 1976): 625.

9. Wald, "State Intervention"; Institute for Judicial Administration—American Bar Association (IJA-ABA), Juvenile Justice Standards Project, *Standards Relating to Abuse and Neglect* (Cambridge, Mass.: Ballinger Publishing Co., 1981).

10. Joseph Goldstein et al., *Beyond the Best Interest of the Child*, p. 9.

11. The prointervention view is argued forcefully by Sanford N. Katz, *When Parents Fail: The Law's Response to Family Breakdown* (Boston: Beacon Press, 1971).

12. Institute of Judicial Administration—American Bar Association (IJA-ABA), Juvenile Justice Standards Project, *Standards Relating to Abuse and Neglect*.

13. IJA-ABA *Standards Relating to Abuse and Neglect* (Cambridge, Mass.: Ballinger Publishing Co., 1977), tentative draft. See also Stanley Fisher, "Parents' Rights and Juvenile Court Jurisdiction: A Review of *Before the Best Interests of the Child*," *American Bar Foundation Research Journal*, Summer 1981, no. 3, p. 838.

14. Norman A. Polansky et al., *Damaged Parents: An Anatomy of Child Neglect* (Chicago: University of Chicago Press, 1981), pp. 159–175.

15. Representative George Miller (D., Cal.), who chairs the House Select Committee on Children, Youth, and Families, created in February 1983, will have the advantage of a forum from which to raise similar issues. As a select committee, Miller's committee cannot sponsor legislation, however. See Steven V. Roberts's "Now, a Select Committee for Families," The *New York Times*, February 23, 1983, p. A-19.

16. *Child Protection Report*, May 7, 1982, pp. 3–4.

17. John W. Ellwood, "Controlling the Growth of Federal Domestic Spending," in John W. Ellwood, ed., *Reductions in U.S. Domestic Spending: How They Affect State and Local Governments* (New Brunswick, N.J.: Transaction Books, 1982), p. 8.

18. Allen Schick, "Reconciliation and the Congressional Budget Process" (Washington, D.C.: American Enterprise Institute, Congress Project, May 20, 1981), p. 38.

19. The "Teenage Chastity Act" was enacted through the 1981 Omnibus Reconciliation Act, but no funds were appropriated.

Index

Abbott, Grace, 149 n.41

Advisory Council on Child Welfare Services, 1960, Fred DelliQuadri, 45. *See also* Social Security Act, Maternal and Child Welfare Amendments to, 1960–63

Agenda setting, 20–31; conflicts in, 106–12; and Children's Bureau, 128; and Congress, 98–103, 121–25, 134–36; definition of, 20–22, 25, 126; economic approaches to, 29–31; formal agenda (governmental or public), 20; governmental, 126–37; and initial maintenance, 23; and issue careers, 25; and issue clusters, 25; and issue cycles, 25; and liberal reform, 136–37; media and, 51–75, 129–23; organizational approach to, 21–23; and recurring maintenance, 23; stages of, 22–23; and state legislatures, 132–34; systemic agenda (popular or professional), 20; valence issues in, 93–94

Allen, John T., 106

American Academy of Pediatrics, 132; model child abuse statute of, 3

American Humane Association (AHA), ix; 42, 86, 132; child protective services, 40–41, 44; definition of, 2–3; Children's Division, 39–41; and Vincent De Francis, 40–41; and newspapers, 65–66

American Law Institute (ALI), 82

American Medical Association, and birth registration, 37, 132

American Public Health Association, and birth registration, 37

American Public Nurse Association, 41

American Society for the Prevention of Cruelty to Animals, Henry Berg, 7–8

Anti-interventionist concerns, and child reporting laws, 90–91

Ariès, Phillipe, 6

Bain, Katherine, 60

"Battered-Child Syndrome, The," 72, 129, 130; definition of, 13; C. Henry Kempe, 13, 16, 43; and the media, 56, 58–60, 63, 65

Bauer, Raymond, 26

Before the Best Interests of the Child, 90

Bendener, Robert, 95

Bergh, Henry, 55; and American Society for the Prevention of Cruelty to Animals, 7–8

Berman, Daniel, 95

Beyond the Best Interests of thes36Child, 90–91

Biaggi, Mario, 92, 97, 98–99, 102, 113, 134

Bible, Alan, 98

Billingsley, Andrew, 47

Bill of Rights, extended to children, *In re Gault* opinion, 12, 40–41

Birch, Tom, 120

Borcherding, Thomas E., 29

Brademas, John, 99; and Child Abuse Prevention and Treatment Act, 112, 115–16

Bureau of the Census, and birth registration, 37

Caffey, John, 12

Carstens, C. C., Massachusetts Society for the Prevention of Cruelty to Children, 10

Child Abuse: and Aid to Dependent Children, 152 n.39; in American Gilded Age, 5; and Children's Bureau, 39–50; congressional response to, 98–103; as deviance, 3, 136; difficulty of measuring, 15–17; listed in *Annual Reports* of the U.S. Children's Bureau, 41–42; *Index Medi-*

Index

Index

Protective custody, 132–34; and child abuse reporting laws, 89–90

Public use of private deviance, 3, 17–19, 51, 124, 126–37

Race, 15

Racism, 90, 136

Randolph, Jennings, 108; and Child Abuse Prevention Act, 1–2

Rape, 3, 124, 127; anti-rape movement, 65

Reagan, Ronald, 81, 119, 120, 129; cuts in social programs, 3

Rockefeller, Nelson, 81

Rogers, Everett, 77

Roosevelt, Franklin D., 37

Roosevelt, Theodore, 34–35

Rosenthal, Alan, 83

Salisbury, Robert H., 26

Santosky vs. Kramer, 91

Saturday Evening Post, and child abuse, 60

Schattschneider, E. E, 3, 26

Schick, Allen, 123, 135

Schroeder, Patricia, 97, 99, 113, 159 n.40

Schweiker, Lonnie, 120

Schweiker, Richard, 120

Scientific Charity Movement, 9, 53, 55

Senate, U.S., and child abuse reporting laws, 104–12

Sexual child abuse, 3, 124, 127

Sheppard-Tower Infancy and Maternity Act, 37, 39. *See also* Children's Bureau

Shoemaker, F. Floyd, 77

Shorter, Edward, 6

Silverman, Frederic N., 60, 82

Smelser, Neil, 5

Social and Rehabilitative Services, Children's Bureau under, 48

Social problem, definition of, 5

Socialism, ix, 18–19

Social Security Act: Maternal and Child Welfare Amendments to, 1960–63, 39, 45, 46; 1962 Amendments to, 12; 1967 Amendments to, 49; Title XX Amendment to (1974), 109–11

Solnit, Albert J., 90

Some Ethical Gains through Legislation (Florence Kelley), 34

Spector, Malcolm, 22

Stafford, Robert T., 108, 112, 119

Steiner, Gilbert Y., 16, 37

Stibitz, Charles, 70. *See also* Cheryl Ann Tabor

Stibitz, Mary, 70. *See also* Cheryl Ann Tabor

Stone, Clement, 120

Stone, Donna, 120

Stone, Lawrence, 6

Sugarman, Jule M., and Children's Bureau, 38

Switzer, Mary E., and Children's Bureau, 38, 48

Tabor, Cheryl Ann, 69, 70–71

Taft, William Howard: Children's Bureau, 35

Teenage Chastity Act, 162 n.19

Television and child abuse, 56–57

Thomas, Stanley, 115, 135

Time magazine, and "Battered-Child Syndrome," 60, 152 n.33

Trenton Evening Times, 70

Truman, Harry S., and Children's Bureau, 37

Tuchman, Gaye, 72

Typology of Legislative Processes (Michael T. Hayes), 26

United Community Chests and Councils of America, 41

Uslaner, Eric M., 96

Violence against Children (David Gil), 44

Violence issues, 27–29, 90, 94, 111; defined, 27, 127

Violence, social, 3, 9, 17–19. *See also* Child abuse; Domestic violence; Incest; Neglect; Rape; Sexual child abuse

Wald, Lillian, and Children's Bureau, 33–34

Wald, Michael S., 90, 156 n.44

Walker, Jack L., 81, 154 n.13

Walkowitz, Judy, 150 n.12

168

Index

War on Poverty, 12

Weicker, Lowell, 119

Weinberger, Caspar, 116

Wheeler, Etta Angell, and "Mary Ellen" case, 7

White House Conference on Dependent Children, 1909, 10, 84

Wilkinson, Tom, 52

Wilson, Fanny, and "Mary Ellen" case, 7

Wilson, Mary Ellen, 54, 67–68, 70–71, 127. *See also* "Mary Ellen" case

Woolley, P. V., 12, 58

Young, Leontine, 86